CANADIAN CASH MANAGEMENT: A GUIDE TO FINANCIAL STRATEGIES

CANADIAN CASH MANAGEMENT: A GUIDE TO FINANCIAL STRATEGIES

Jeffrey D. Sherman, B.Comm, M.B.A., F.C.S.I., C.A.

THOMSON

™

CARSWELL

National Library of Canada Cataloguing in Publication

Sherman. Jeffrey D.
   Canadian cash management: a guide to financial strategies / Jeffrey D. Sherman.

Includes index.
ISBN 0-459-28009-0

   1. Cash management—Canada. I. Title.

HG4028.C45S535 2003   658.15'244   C2003-905051-3

THOMSON

CARSWELL

One Corporate Plaza
2075 Kennedy Road
Toronto, Ontario
M1T 3V4

Customer Relations:
Toronto 416-609-3800
Elsewhere in Canada/U.S. 1-800-387-5164
Fax 416-298-5082

PREFACE

In the 21st century, the finance function is vital to the success of any business. Strong controls, effective budgeting, tight credit and collection will make your business more effective and efficient. *Canadian Cash Management: A Guide to Financial Strategies* is designed to be a reference for CFOs, treasurers, controllers, accounting managers and their staff.

This book contains concise, up-to-date and practical information on:

- Financial strategy
- Improving credit and collections
- Strengthening internal controls
- Understanding e-commerce and electronic payments
- Forecasting and budgeting
- Improving cash management

Canadian Cash Management is based upon *Canadian Treasury Management*, a comprehensive guide to financial and treasury management in Canada. Our readers have asked for a smaller, more concise reference covering specifically financial and cash management. Consequently, *Canadian Cash Management* is a reprint of the chapters from the larger book devoted to financial strategy, budgeting and cash management.

Chapter 4 — "E-Commerce and E-Payments" is written by Craigg Ballance, one of the leading experts on electronic payments and commerce in Canada.

We would like to hear from any readers with comments or suggestions to improve future editions of this book. Please e-mail *jdsherman@sympatico.ca*, or fax to (416) 736-0881.

Jeffrey D. Sherman
Toronto, October 2003

ABOUT THE AUTHOR
AND CONTRIBUTING WRITER

Jeffrey D. Sherman, B.Comm., M.B.A., C.A., (author) has written extensively on contemporary finance, business and accounting issues. He has over 20 years business experience as chief financial officer of both public and private companies, as a consultant specializing in corporate finance, and has worked for a large chartered bank in various senior capacities. Mr. Sherman has lectured and conducted seminars on finance, accounting, derivatives and information technology for many organizations, and he was an adjunct professor at York University. His books include *Migration Canada* (published by Kluwer), a guide to the tax and legal implications of moving into or out of Canada, and *Financial Instruments: A Guide for Financial Managers* (Carswell).

Craigg Ballance (Chapter 4 — "E-Commerce and E-Payments") has been managing technology and business convergence in the financial arena for over 20 years. He is recognized as an expert in the area of electronic business and payments processes and is the co-author of three books: *Electronic Commerce Relationships: Trust by Design* (Prentice Hall) focused on building trust, security and effective control in EC, *On-Line Profits: A Manager's Guide to Electronic Commerce* (Harvard Business Press) and *Electronic Commerce and EDI in the Financial Industry* (Lafferty Publications). Over the past decade, Mr. Ballance has provided consulting and design expertise to numerous banking and corporate organizations around the world, as well as in Canada — helping apply technology and electronic payment methodologies. He is a partner with E-Finity Group Inc. in Toronto.

TABLE OF CONTENTS

DETAILED TABLE OF CONTENTS

DETAILED TABLE OF CONTENTS

C H A P T E R 1

Financial Strategy

Overview

In theory, the objective of the business enterprise is to maximize shareholder wealth. In practice, however, the relationship between management decisions and changes in shareholder wealth are often unclear. This chapter suggests that the use of clear goals and objectives will result in an improved financial performance and a higher value for the business.

Corporate Mission and Financial Objectives

Every business organization has a mission that indicates why it exists. There may be a formal mission statement, clearly laid out and widely understood by shareholders and employees. The mission of the enterprise may be obvious and implicit. Or, as is more often the case, the mission may be unclear. In the latter case, if pressed, management might suggest that the mission of the business is to survive, to achieve ever increasing levels of profitability, or some meaningless aphorism. But every business does have a mission, whether clear or cloudy, useful or pointless.

Business objectives should be set by senior management as a means of fulfilling the mission of the enterprise. At the level of the overall business, the objectives should be broad and clear and also permit assessment as to when and how they are achieved. Objectives commonly will relate to various functional areas. For example, there may be objectives relating to marketing and sales, customer service, production, human resources, and shareholder relations. There may be specific financial objectives to guide the enterprise in the short-, medium- or long-term.

Regardless of objectives otherwise determined, every business enterprise has a fundamental financial objective — the maximization of shareholders' wealth. Absent that as a financial objective, the corporation may be focused excessively on perpetuating management rather than benefitting shareholders. Since shareholders have the ultimate ownership interest in the corporation, the focus on their well-being is appropriate. In financial terms, well-being equates to maximizing wealth.

The notion of risk and return is often implied in a company's strategy. High returns are associated with risky strategies, moderate returns with less risky strategies. Similarly, returns may be more or less volatile, depending upon the strategy followed.

Shareholder Wealth

Shareholder wealth is increased by maximizing the amount of cash flow ultimately accruing to the shareholders. This cash flow originates from two sources: dividends paid out by the corporation, and increases in the market value of the corporation (that is, an increase in the value of common shares). Cash flow in the business can be distributed to investors through dividends or the repurchase of shares, or it can be retained in the business to generate sales and income growth, thus presumably increasing share values in the long run. Income, as measured by generally accepted accounting principles, is the normal measure of cash flows actually earned by the business.

In public corporations, as well as other corporations where management is separate from share ownership, the managers are agents of the shareholders. That is, they work for and on behalf of shareholders. If the shareholders were polled, it is unlikely that they could agree upon any overall corporate objective other than that of shareholder wealth maximization. Secondary objectives such as being a good corporate citizen or minimizing pollution can only endure if the business itself is profitable and thriving.

Literature on management often refers to *stakeholders* to describe the various parties with an interest in a business enterprise. Stakeholders include shareholders, employees, creditors, customers, suppliers, governments, and even the public. It is unlikely that all of these stakeholders would agree on corporate objectives. Since the owners of the business probably would agree on the financial objective of maximizing their wealth, this focus appears defensible.

While the financial objective of generating shareholder wealth is simple to state, it is not in itself terribly useful as a plan for action. The relationship between management decisions and changes in shareholder wealth is generally uncertain and unpredictable. Nonetheless, attention to shareholder wealth provides a useful focus for evaluating financial strategies and policies.

Planning and Maximizing Share Price

An increase in share price is one element of maximizing shareholder wealth. (The other is dividends.) In addition to benefitting shareholders directly, appreciating share prices have other beneficial effects on the business enterprise:

- Improving access to capital;
- Facilitating the acquisition process;
- Improving the ability to resist being acquired;
- Management retention and compensation;
- Relations with creditors; and
- Relations with shareholders.

Therefore, corporate financial strategy should be designed to have a positive impact on the share price. In the case of private corporations, increases in the market value and marketability of the corporation overall have the same effect as an increase in the share price of a publicly traded corporation.

The simplest measure of share price is the market to book ratio. This is the ratio of share price to book value per share, or the ratio of the market value of the entire company to its book value. In either case, book value refers to shareholders' equity accruing to the common shareholders: that is, common share capital, paid in capital and other surplus, and retained earnings.

In theory, a market to book ratio of greater than 1.0 suggests that every dollar put up by the equity holders has been transformed by management into a market value of more than a dollar.

Similarly, a market to book ratio of less than 1.0 indicates that management has destroyed value.

The use of differing accounting policies will significantly influence market to book ratios. Even different accounting practices within a policy have significant effect. For example, fixed assets might be depreciated over 10 years or 30 years. While such variations in practice should be based upon differing factual situations, that is not always the case.

Another difficulty with the market to book ratio is that financial accounting does not track fair values, rather it simply records actual dollars expended. The impact of inflation or changes in purchasing power is not taken into account.

A related problem is that analysis of the process of creating value or destroying value must be done based on incremental effects. For example, a company may have a low market to book ratio as a result of poor management decisions historically. The relevant measure is the impact of the current management decisions on improving the market to book ratio. When evaluating a real company, it can be difficult to disentangle the impact of old and new decisions upon the market to book ratio.

The market to book ratio is a measure for evaluating how cheap or expensive the shares or market price of a company will be. The market value itself is ultimately based upon future cash flows and it can be instructive to analyze those cash flows themselves.

The market price of a company is based upon the future income stream (cash flows) expected to accrue to shareholders. Those cash flows must be discounted at an appropriate interest rate to determine their present value. As a practical matter, cash flows and discount rate are very difficult to determine, although their theoretical components can readily be analyzed.

Expected income stream or cash flows depends upon projected profitability and growth. The appropriate discount rate to discount the stream is based upon risk considerations as well as overall economic outlook. Putting those factors together, it can be seen that share prices can be enhanced by altering numerous factors:

- Expected sales growth rate;
- Expected operating profit growth;
- Expected investment in working capital and capital assets (fixed assets);
- Current interest rates and cost of capital; and
- General economic outlook.

Some of these cannot be influenced by the company itself. Nonetheless, they are important considerations in arriving at a strategic plan. Other factors should form part of the overall corporate objectives and then help drive the strategic plan itself.

The Central Role of Financial Objectives

For better or worse, accounting provides the language and primary means of evaluation in the modern business environment. Facts, transactions and items are recorded in terms of money. That is, things that are purchased and tangible are accounted for. Events are ignored if they don't have immediate monetary impact. Assets or liabilities not acquired from outsiders, that are not tangible and paid for, or that represent future commitments ("executory contracts") are not effectively measured and recorded by the accounting system. Therefore, most companies have relatively poor information on such items as internally developed goodwill, environmental damage or liabilities.

Financial accounting measures are nonetheless useful in setting clear and unambiguous objectives and in permitting their evaluation.

Using Financial Goals

An example of the implementation of financial policy, and its useful-ness in setting quantifiable goals, is set out below. A useful summary measure of the effectiveness of an enterprise is return on capital employed ("ROCE"). ROCE is net income divided by capital employed. It is often derived by considering two related measures, profit on sales and capital turnover:

$$\text{ROCE} \;=\; \%\ \text{profit on sales} \times \text{capital turnover ratio}$$

$$=\; \frac{\text{net income}}{\text{sales}} \;\times\; \frac{\text{sales}}{\text{capital employed}}$$

$$=\; \frac{\text{net income}}{\text{capital employed}}$$

ROCE is normally examined by considering its trend over time, comparing it to what should be theoretically possible or desirable given the nature of the enterprise, and by comparing it to plan. The equations above can be used to break it into components:

- *Net income*, which depends upon gross margin on sales, the relationship between gross margin (total contribution) and fixed costs, and taxation; and
- *Capital employed*, which is net working capital (current assets less current liabilities) plus non-current assets (in general, primarily fixed assets).

The profit on sales ratio measures the amount of net income generated by each dollar of revenue. Capital turnover indicates the level of sales that $1 of capital employed will support.

Thus, ROCE could be increased by any or all of the following strategies:

- Increase sales volumes (keeping fixed costs the same);
- Increase the gross margin on sales (keeping sales volumes constant);
- Reduce the level of capital employed (while keeping sales constant);
- Increase sales volumes (by keeping capital employed constant); or
- Reduce income taxes (assuming no change to income before taxes).

Sales volume is the domain of marketing policy. Margins, cost structures, and productivity are influenced by operations management. The level of capital employed may be influenced by operations management (for example, inventory control). However, the primary determinant of the amount of capital employed is financial policy. Thus, financial policy itself will directly affect ROCE. The level and use of capital in business enterprises are discussed in more detail below.

The ratio of net income to sales may be further analyzed using various measures. A particularly interesting one is to relate it to measures based on the number of employees. For example:

$$\frac{\text{Net income}}{\text{Sales}} = \frac{\text{net income}}{\text{headcount}} \Big/ \frac{\text{sales}}{\text{headcount}}$$

Headcount can be measured as "full time equivalent" (FTE) staff, or any other measure that tracks the level of employment.

This approach tracks net income per employee — a powerful measure of the overall effectiveness of the organization — and also tracks sales per employee, a good measure of efficiency. This is particularly interesting when comparing the results of different business units within the same organization. In addition, sudden or unexpected changes in these measures may be leading indicators of problems.

Cost of Capital and Rate Of Return

The minimum acceptable return from a project is the rate of inter-est that the firm is paying for the capital invested in it. A firm draws capital from various sources and each has a different cost. The objective should be to develop a financing structure that min-imizes the firm's weighted average cost of capital.

The cost of capital in capital budgeting processes is the hurdle against which investment alternatives are judged.

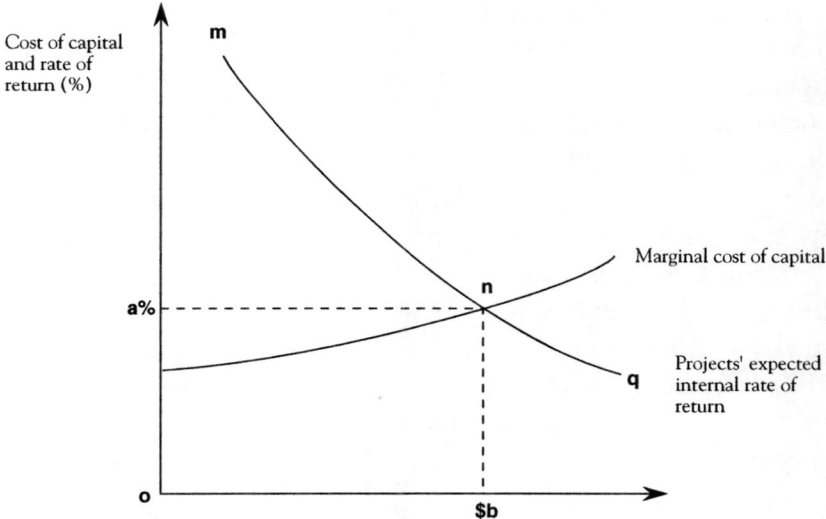

Projects falling on the curve m – n would be undertaken, as their forecasted return exceeds the cost of capital a%. The capital budget needed to finance is $b. Projects falling on the curve n – q would be rejected, as their return would not cover cost of capital of a%.

Capital budgeting and the financial structure of the firm (the mix between equity and debt) cannot be viewed in isolation from each other. Changes in financial structure will affect cost of capital calculations, and vice versa. As the proportion of debt increases relative to equity, there is a greater probability that earnings per share and return to equity will vary from one year to another. The more debt there is to service, the less profit there is to distribute to shareholders. The result may be an increase in the rate of return required by holders of equity, or the lowering of share prices.

At the same time, the cost of debt may rise at an increasing rate as the leverage ratio increases. This may in part be due to the need to use a variety of debt sources, some of which may charge different interest rates. It will also be due to risk assessments made by sources of loan finance who may consider that the more debt the firm has, the higher the interest requirements, and the higher the interest charges, the greater the probability that earnings will not always be sufficient to meet these charges. Risk premiums may be the result. We can describe this dilemma in terms of cash-flow ability to service debt. When considering the appropriate capital structure, it is important to analyze the cash flow (capacity) of the firm to service fixed charges. The greater and more stable the expected future cash flows of the firm, the greater the debt capacity of the firm.

Control of Working Capital and Cash Flow

The maintenance of satisfactory cash flows is always an important objective. Working capital is the ratio of current assets to current liabilities. The acid test ratio is:

$$\frac{\text{current assets minus inventories and prepaids}}{\text{current liabilities}} = \frac{\text{liquid assets}}{\text{current liabilities}}$$

FINANCIAL STRATEGY

The control of working capital is the key to the maintenance of cash flows which are positive (i.e., net inflows) at the time they are needed. Such control may be obtained under three headings:

- *Sufficient working capital* such that the business can cope with volume and inflationary increases in the cost of its inputs. A situation of negative cash flow (i.e., net outflows) will lead to an increase in current liabilities, a situation which trade creditors and the bank will eventually restrict in their own interest. This risk can only be offset by having positive incoming cash flows with which to offset any imbalance between current assets and the current liabilities, preferably at least to a point where the acid test ratio shows a balance between liquid assets and current liabilities plus imminent outgoings, such as for payments of interest on longer-term loans.

- *Working capital turnover* — The flow of working capital, particularly cash, is summarized below. The speed of the flow is important. The faster it goes, the greater the output that may be obtained from expensive fixed assets, and the smaller the investment in working capital needed to obtain this output. At the same time, the business must seek to prevent the unnecessary build up of working capital within the cycle, by monitoring stock levels and debtors.

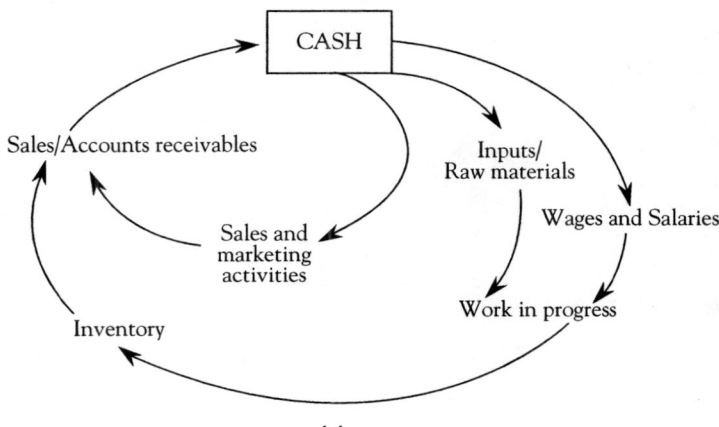

- Product life cycle — Analysis of the product mix relative to positions on product life cycle may show which products should be producing positive cash flows and which are not, especially when there is a heavy demand for cash to finance new product development.

Controls, Systems and Budgets

Overview

The purpose of controls and systems is to ensure that performance is optimized. The control system is not an end in itself — a truism that sometimes is forgotten.

The discussion in this chapter relates primarily to feedback controls and the use of the control system to enhance performance in real time.

Management controls — regardless of their type — seek to ensure that performance conforms to plans. This entails an iterative process of evaluating performance and taking corrective measures when performance differs from plans. There are three phases to the management control process:

- establishing standards;
- measuring performance against standards; and
- correcting deviations from standards.

The Control Process

Controls can be classified according to function and timing:

- *Feedback controls* detect deviations from the standard and provide for corrective measures to be taken before the operation is completed.
- *Approval procedures* require that approval be obtained before a next step can be taken.
- *After-the-fact controls* measure results after the operation is completed.

Establishing standards

The control process begins with plans. In the planning process, there is a continuous narrowing of detail from specific tactical plans to broad strategies. The tactical plans establish goals, targets, and standards to guide the fulfilment of strategic plans.

Managerial decision is important at this point in choosing and defining specific standards to guide action. The key to determining what standards will be set is the answer to the question: what is it that management wishes to measure? Standards cannot be set for everything so choices must be made about those key activities that managers wish to monitor continuously.

The "80/20" rule can be an important guideline. In 1906, an Italian economist Vilfredo Pareto described the unequal distribution of wealth in Italy, and noted that 20 per cent of the people owned 80 per cent of the wealth. Since then, this observation has been applied (somewhat illogically) to many other areas, and it stands for the proposition that 20 per cent of something may be responsible for 80 per cent of the results. So, 20 per cent of customers yield 80 per cent of the profits, 20 per cent of inventory takes up 80 per cent of warehouse space, 20 per cent of employees account for 80 per cent of absences, and so on. The 80/20 rule is not an immutable law; rather, it is a reminder that a few things will account for most of the results. The converse also applies: 80 per cent of something will account for only 20 per cent of the results.

Measuring performance against standards

There are many important facets to the measurement of performance. First, how much variation will constitute a reason for taking corrective action? Second, managers must be on the alert to determine whether standards should be altered. As changes in the environment take place, it may be necessary to correct standards before looking at performance. Variable budgets are designed to do precisely this. Third, management must develop the proper type of reporting and information system to appraise, compare, and correct performance. This aspect of control opens up a vast subject because it concerns not only control but all other aspects of management as well. As far as control is concerned, the management information system must identify those points in a manager's area of responsibility, the surveillance of which will permit the manager to exercise the appropriate control over employee performance in achieving the targets for which the manager is responsible. This is a complex design problem because it must be responsive to a manager's needs, knowledge, preferred methods to get and use information, the standard under review, and so on. The less concrete the standard against which performance is measured, the more difficult the information system design problem.

Control reports will vary at different levels in the organization. The chief executive officer, for instance, will want reports concerned with whether the missions and objectives of the company are still adequate, whether critical parts of the strategic plan are being implemented (for example, acquisitions, divestitures, new product development, and progress of new facility construction), and whether current operations are satisfactory. The executive vice-president will want more penetrating details about the operations of the enterprise, and the focus of lower level managers will be narrower.

Reports that compare actual results with desired results may be useful for certain types of information but inadequate for others. When managers are appraising the overall performance of other managers, a comparison of financial results of their area of operation with predetermined objectives is a needed base for evaluation. For many other types of activities, however, what is required is advance warning, or predictors of results. This is future-oriented, feedforward, control. Managers do not want to find out that sales last month were 10 per cent under what was desired. They want to know today that sales next month may be 10 per cent under standard unless some action is taken to counter the trend. Really effective control requires accurate prediction.

Ingenuity is needed to find useful predictors. Forecasts provide one type of forewarning. A sales manager may use a composite of field visits, customer inquiries, complaints, returned merchandise, and so on, to foresee future deviations from plans.

Evaluating performance and taking corrective action

Measurements of past performances and predictions of things to come alert management to what is going on or likely to happen but do not determine what should be done. There are two phases to this activity. The first concerns the evaluation of the warning signals, and the second relates to managerial decision about any remedies for correcting deviations for standards.

Proper evaluation of signals is important. Some methods to predict future events may not be entirely reliable and considerable judgment may be required to prevent precipitous action. For example, a sudden increase in the sale of a product may indicate a fad and not a long-lived increase in consumer demand. To take action on the current jump in sales could lead to excessive overcapacity, rising costs per unit, and declining profits.

Once a manager decides that corrective action is required, the issue then joins the entire process of management. A revision of plans may be required. New standards may be needed. Better motivation of employees may be desired, and so on. Although control may be identified as a key function of managers, it cannot be performed without simultaneous actions among other functions.

Effective Budget Systems

Designing and implementing an effective system of controls is complex — more so in larger enterprises. Some guidelines and factors that improve the likelihood of installing a successful and effective budgetary system are set out below.

- There should be support by top management. No control and budget system can be successful without the unqualified support of senior management.

17

- There should be a clear organizational structure. For the budget process to be effective, managers must understand their accountabilities and authority. They need to have clearly defined roles in the organization and fully understand their relationships with peers, subordinates, and superiors in the organization. This is necessary to ensure that the budget covers precisely the responsibilities of each manager.

- The budget system should form part of an effective, company-wide, planning program. It is an integral part of the planning process. The challenge (and duty) of senior management is to convert long-range strategic plans into quantitative budgetary objectives for each business area.

- Responsibility for the budgetary system must be clearly laid out and understood. Although the ultimate responsibility rests with top management, in all but the smallest firms, the task is delegated to someone else, often a comptroller or planning manager. The work of preparing the budget becomes one of collecting, disseminating, organizing, and evaluating information. In larger companies, the precise duties may be set out in a detailed procedural manual.

- Budgets should not dominate the decision-making process. They do not replace the need for judgment by managers. Common sense must be used in day-to-day decision-making. For example, managers should feel comfortable in deviating from budgets if they have valid business reasons. Similarly, the budget should not be used as a reason to be uncooperative with another department. As the environment changes, flexibility may be necessary. The budget should be administered firmly, but also flexibly, when appropriate.

- Keep it simple and easy to understand. Avoid accounting jargon, esoteric language, and arcane criteria.

- Do not let the budget process become overly complex or cumbersome. The budgetary process is a mechanism to delegate authority. If there are detailed restrictions, too much detail, or a confining process, the managers will become frustrated. This will lead to resentment and, probably, bureaucratic inertia. The budget is a tool for management: it is not to be confused with management itself.

- State measurement criteria clearly. The budget process will work better if budgets have clearly defined standards to measure performance. The advantage of clear standards is that exceptions can be reported objectively, and appropriate follow-up measures can be taken. Alternatively, superior performance can be noted objectively, and appropriate action can be taken. All of this will result in the process being perceived as fair, which will improve buy-in to the process by managers and staff.

- There must be adequate understanding of the purpose and limitations of the budget throughout the enterprise. Budgets are tools to help the company achieve its objectives. They are not meant to frustrate or annoy, as lower-level managers in some companies feel. Budgets should not be used to pressure unduly or to goad employees to higher levels of performance.

- Discourage game-playing with budgets. For example, extra spending at the end of the fiscal year to ensure a higher base for the following year's budget should be discouraged. There are two general ways to do this. One is by having a corporate culture in which such games are simply not considered appropriate. The other (related) technique is to follow the guidelines laid down here. If the budgetary process is perceived as being fair and equitable, then there will be buy-in and it will be used effectively by both managers and employees.

- There should be widespread participation in the development of the budget. People generally do not like budgets, since they do not like to be controlled. By involving as many as possible in the development of the budget, the constraints resulting from it become more palatable. Another subtle benefit often results: as more people understand the overall organizational objectives and constraints, they can better appreciate the reasons for their own budgetary goals.

- The budgetary system should be economical. It should be cheap to operate with the minimum number of controls and reports, yet still be effective. The system should be kept as simple as possible. The cost of a control or report versus the benefits resulting therefrom should be a major consideration.

- Budgets should be meaningful. Budgets should be established only for the important things that management wishes to measure, monitor, and understand. This is closely related to the accounting concept of "materiality". Something is material if it can influence the action taken by a decision-maker. If an item is not material, the budget should ignore it. Note that materiality depends not only on the absolute dollar amount, but also the nature of the item. An increase of $10,000 in total salary costs may be immaterial to the budget, whereas the same increase in promotional expense may be material. The operational consideration is whether the decision-maker may take action based upon the item. (Materiality is not a number that is *set*, rather it is *discovered*, based upon the behaviour of people.)

- The budgetary system must be tailored to the enterprise. There is no one ideal budgeting, suitable for all organizations. The unique characteristics of a company, including ownership, management style, size, problems, purpose, and environment all enter into the design.

- It will often be beneficial to have both a budget, which is fixed for the year, and a rolling estimate of what results are likely to be.

Company Size

There are significant differences in control systems between large and small companies. In very small companies, relatively few budgets and tactical plans are required because managers are in constant contact with each other and their employees. The production process, marketing considerations, cash flow analysis, etc., tend to be much simpler than in a larger enterprise. Therefore, it is easier to manage and monitor the company without an elaborate reporting system.

In larger organizations, communication problems between managers at all levels become more difficult to resolve. It becomes more difficult to co-ordinate activities. As a result, the budgetary system frequently plays a major role in operating the business and assisting communications between managers. Larger organizations are also subject to more external threats and require a wider network of scanning techniques to anticipate the threats. As a result, control systems in larger companies are more complex.

Cost of Management Information

Time

The value of any piece of information is related to time. The most simplistic view taken is that the value of the information reduces as time passes. This implies, however, acceptance of one of the myths of information — that the quicker the information is available the greater its value. The true relationship of time to information is more complex than this. This relationship depends upon the type of decision to be taken. There are three categories: decisions that are improved by the speed of information flow, those that are unaffected by it, and those that are actually hindered.

The simple relationship, where the value of information is corelated to time, applies to the first type of decision — for example, control information. Even in this case, however, it would be pertinent to analyze the cost of not having the information, which increases as time increases. Strictly speaking, this will be the case when the process is not in control. When the process is in control, the value of the control information is limited, but the purpose of control information is to monitor.

In a complex decision, there may be a series of sub-decisions, each of which involves gathering of information. Some information may be used to determine further information requirements. Information for this type of decision could have a value time relationship. This cannot be considered a general pattern as the value may fall between the two decisions or it may increase for the second decision or it may decrease. It will become more complicated as more decisions are involved with the piece of information.

A decision may be hindered by timely data if the data is highly variable. Highly variable data requires the passage of time to determine the extent of the variability.

An example of this is found in process control. The output of a production process is monitored to ensure that items produced are acceptable. Some process control systems have fixed time interval sampling of the process, others have a variable time interval sampling. With the variable time interval sampling, the sampling will be carried out at a fixed time interval until it is thought the process is going out of control. The time interval will then be reduced to check on the process. If it is out of control then this will be rectified, and if a false alarm has occurred then the fixed time interval sampling will be resumed. With examples of this type, the timing of the information becomes more important when there are indications the process is out of control.

Knowledge

Knowledge can be defined as the body of facts relating to the principles and practices of management and any related facts necessary for the successful management of an organization. It would be foolish to consider that every manager would personally know all of this knowledge, but it would not seem unreasonable to suggest that a manager should be able to have access to this knowledge through the management team of an organization and through management education.

Knowledge determines the extent to which the information approaches its true value. It does not add to the true value of the information, but a lack of it does not allow the true value to be achieved. An individual's perception of his state of knowledge is not necessarily reliable. Individuals may have a pessimistic or an optimistic view of their state of knowledge.

The factor of knowledge is extremely important when talking in terms of information needs because there is no point in providing information if the knowledge as to how to use it is absent. It would therefore seem reasonable that the information analyst should provide access to the knowledge as well as the information.

Prior information

In determining the value of a piece of information, all the other information connected with it must be considered — for example, a company must decide whether or not to carry out a market survey into the sales of a commodity. The value of the information produced will be affected by the information already available. If the product is new, and no other sales information is available, the value of such a survey in most cases will be more than if the product is an established one with past sales figures which can be used to forecast. The factor that could reverse this relationship could be termed the surprise factor. The larger the surprise factor of a piece of information the greater the value of that piece of information.

Accuracy

The greater the accuracy of a piece of information the greater its value; however, the law of diminishing returns applies. There are a number of cases where accuracy is of great importance, especially at the operational level. There are also quite a number of cases where absolute accuracy is both unnecessary and possibly misleading.

Accuracy is also related to time and cost. As a general principle, the greater the accuracy required the more time and/or cost will be incurred. If information is being prepared for a time-dependent decision, the level of accuracy and/or cost could well be forced on the manager by the time constraint.

Quantity

The amount of information can affect its value. If the quantity of information is so large as to overload the manager, the value may be reduced. All managers suffer under a time constraint; therefore, there is a chance that some of the value of a large amount of information may be lost because of insufficient time to study it. If a large number of pieces of information are provided for a particular decision or series of decisions there can be a similar effect.

Power

Managers will use some information to create uncertainty rather than to reduce it. Information may not be the only source of a manager's power in the organization, but it is certainly an effective one. The power may be exercised by information being released selectively, slowly, or not at all.

Using Management Information Systems Effectively

The budget and control system is an integral part of management information systems. Computers are almost invariably used in this process. The degree of sophistication used in practice is enormous. At one end of the spectrum, a spreadsheet summarizing budget versus actual results may be prepared, using manual input, by a clerk. At the other extreme, a thousand-person systems department may generate hundreds of thousands of pages of data monthly to help in the management process. It is a supreme irony of this information age that many managers in the latter case might have been better served by a one-page spreadsheet, which they do indeed sometimes produce themselves by keying in data manually.

Much has been written about how to control management information systems. Several recurring themes are set out below:

- *Focus constantly on profits, otherwise you won't get them* — Sometimes, the system overwhelms the managers. Many computer systems conversions of the 60s and 70s failed because the technology became an end in itself, rather than a means to improve operations and, consequently, profitability.

- *Any activity managed on the basis of technical criteria will be unprofitable* — The easiest mistake made in managing systems is to treat the function differently from any other. Certainly, the systems function is an unusual blend of development and production, all too often with a bit of research thrown in, but it presents no new problems to the experienced manager. Developing computer systems involves complex design decisions and trade-offs, in which many of the parameters are uncertain. The technology involved is developing so rapidly that even full-time systems people have to restrict their view in order to cope with the range of options. When executives become unhappy at the cost of or poor contribution of the systems department, it is easy to be lured into discussing technical alternatives and specific application problems. Once that happens they are lost. The executives may understand enough, or believe they do, to become advocates of one solution or another. They may, on the other hand, find the detail and its complexity hopelessly confusing. Either way, the technology is fascinating, and they will have joined the alligator-fighters. The swamp will remain undrained. The management role in systems is the same as anywhere else: set the right objectives, monitor performance, and insist on results. Above all, management should demand that solutions to problems be stated in non-technical terms.

- *Any organization, system or procedure left undisturbed for three years will become inefficient* — The scope for improving performance in each area of an organization's activities would normally be identified as the first step in a full information strategy study. This would be followed by an assessment of the quality of the existing systems and the preparation of a future systems plan. The effectiveness of current technology and development techniques would be audited, and a cost, benefit and risk analysis prepared. The conduct of an information strategy study has many other aspects and benefits; however, it is possible to form a quick assessment of the health of a company's systems using only three criteria.

  (a) *Effectiveness* — Are systems having a visible and significant effect on the largest costs, or promoting the biggest revenue earners? Are they doing more than saving heads and automating paperwork? Do managers rely on them for monitoring and control? Are they giving the company an edge over its competition? If the answer to these questions is generally "No", opportunities are being missed.

  (b) *Economy* — Has the systems budget formed an increasing percentage of turnover in each of the last three years? Is more than 20 per cent of the budget spent on keeping systems running, rather than on new work? Are developments measuredin years rather than months? If so, resources may well be being wasted through poor techniques or inadequate use of packaged systems.

  (c) *Obsolescence* — Is any development work done by the users of systems for themselves, with English-like languages or other simple tools? Are data processing and office technology part of a single co-ordinated approach? Do micro-computers outnumber non-intelligent terminals? If not, the systems approach may be dated and will prove increasingly expensive each year until it is changed.

- *Left to themselves, people will make their work more complex rather than simpler* — Everybody knows that, however conscientious an employee, the daily pressures on him or her are more personal, more complex, and more trivial than making a profit. Systems staff may be more highly trained than many, but are no different. Therefore, unless their view of their role is suitably shaped by their objectives, the priorities they adopt may be incompatible with those of senior management.

Systems people are mainly motivated to provide a service to their users. They take a professional pride in satisfying as fully as possible the requests of the accountants, buyers, inventory managers, and the occasional executives with whom they deal. Such requests are rarely couched in terms of profit, and if they are, will be overwhelmed by others related to automating paperwork, providing reports, and other secondary activities.

Frequently, the users make greater demands than they realize on the development skills and technology of the systems department, which rises to the challenge. Systems people are something of an elite. Their career prospects and personal esteem can depend on the technical merit, not to say pioneering nature, of the solutions which they produce. The more elaborate, automated and integrated their system, the greater their market value in a highly mobile profession.

- *No justification study will bear any resemblance to the costs and features of the final solution* — Balancing the potential benefits of a system against the dangers of over-complication is something not often attempted. Most often, senior management plays a passive role, with middle-level systems staff and their users agreeing on a need and a solution and submitting a justification of the expenditure for approval. Such justifications can be weak, but they are rarely challenged, because everyone concerned wants to believe in them, or at least to see them accepted.

Common weaknesses in justification studies are:

(a) Only one alternative solution is properly estimated. Second and third choices are either dismissed in a couple of lines or costed very superficially.

(b) An all-or-nothing proposal. The costs and benefits of discrete elements in the solution should be given, so that management can choose to omit an expensive feature.

(c) There is a single cost and often a single benefit figure. Each of these should be ranges, with estimates of the probability of achieving the extremes as well as the middle of the range.

(d) There is no risk analysis. Threats of increased costs or lower benefits should be identified, with actions planned to minimize the risk.

(e) There is no impetus to achieve the benefits. These may be described as "intangible", or expressed in terms which cannot later be used to enforce their achievement. Proposed new staffing or inventory levels, for example, should be related to the level of sales so that changes in the business environment can be suitably compensated for.

29

Even when a proper justification study has been submitted and approved, often no attempt is made to limit the development to that described in the study. All manner of changes in scope or sophistication are allowed to influence the costs adversely, without any measurable effect on the benefits.

- *Nine-tenths of resources will be spent on tasks which have a minimal impact on profitability* — Setting the right objectives is more important to systems profitability than any other factor, including investment. Asking a systems department to "develop a management information system" (or an inventory system, bonds system, etc.) is like saying to an architect, "build a house". Other "objectives" may be added, such as "make it integrated", "do it by the start of the next fiscal year", or "do it for $20,000". This is like telling the architect, "make it a big house, don't give the foundations time to dry out, and make sure it looks nice". Such objectives determine the type of system produced, but do not specify the type of system required.

Senior executives have more information about the performance of the business than anyone in the systems department. They should state the costs to be attacked, the improvements to be gained, and the market or product directions to be supported, in quantified terms.

Useful objectives might be: (1) Increase inventory turnover by 1.5 times per annum; (2) Shorten production lead-times by five working days; (3) Develop point-of-sales systems to support a 50 per cent increase in volume with no increase in costs; and/or (4) Improve the accounts receivable to sales ratio by two weeks.

The objective should be set jointly for the systems department and the user department most affected, with the latter managing the project. By setting quantified objectives, senior management can concentrate attention on the essentials and can indicate what will be regarded as acceptable performance from the development team.

- *Optional extras will double the costs and the time-scale for development* — Even if all other factors have been handled correctly, it is still possible to push a project from profit to loss through poor implementation. Poor planning, organization and control techniques at this stage can double the cost of a system, extend time-scales by years and create a system which does not meet the original objectives.

Good control begins before the development project is even launched, by obtaining satisfactory answers to the following questions:

(a) Is it the right project (in scope, objectives, priority, etc.) at the right time?
(b) Is it achievable or overly ambitious?
(c) Are the risks identified and minimized?
(d) Are the resources available and justified?
(e) Does everyone understand and accept their role in it?
(f) Is the technology being properly handled?
(g) Are the milestones clearly defined and realistic?
(h) Is the project structured to give results as early as possible?
(i) Have any organizational implications been allowed for?

Once launched, a project can acquire a direction and momentum which makes it difficult to steer if the planning has not been reasonably well done. If the scope, objectives and milestones are clearly defined, it is possible to control against these. Most people, however, make the mistake of only controlling against the milestones. This may tell them that the project is late, but not why.

By identifying and justifying every departure from the original scope and objectives as the development proceeds, two things are achieved. First, the new scope, and therefore the new time-scales, are defined, allowing cost and progress to be controlled against them. Second, the overall viability of the project is kept in view, and it becomes apparent early if the cost or impracticality of what is being developed means that its new scope should be reviewed.

Developing profitable systems is always harder than most people expect. It need not be as difficult as many people make it.

CHAPTER 3

Managing Cash

Overview

Cash provides a focal point when analyzing the financial health of a company because of its central role in all business activity.

Traditional cash management comprises managing deposits and disbursements while ensuring adequate control and generating appropriate information. In a broader sense, however, optimizing the use of cash ensures that the business as a whole is operating efficiently. For example, ensuring that the billing cycle is operating quickly to minimize the level of accounts receivable will also improve customer service. Minimizing inventories to conserve corporate cash may have far-reaching effects on the production process.

This chapter presents an overview of cash management from both viewpoints. Other sections of *Canadian Treasury Management* present more information on specific aspects of cash management:

Investing surplus cash — Chapters 6–10

Cash forecasting and budgeting — Chapter 16

E-Commerce and E-Payments — Chapter 14

Credit and collection — Chapter 15

Banking services and relations — Chapters 4–5

Objectives

Cash management has four primary objectives:

1. To have sufficient cash on hand to pay bills and other obligations as they come due.
2. To have extra cash available if required for emergencies or unusual needs.
3. To minimize the amount of cash tied up in the business (primarily in inventory and accounts receivable).
4. To invest surplus cash safely and profitably.

The corporate cash management process consists of:

- planning cash flows;
- forecasting cash flows;
- handling day-to-day cash receipts and disbursements;

- arranging for short-term cash;
- investing surplus cash effectively; and
- dealing with issues related to international cash management, such as foreign exchange.

Cash on Hand

Cash may be held for five primary reasons:

1. *Transactions* — Cash balances are held to conduct day-to-day business activity. Payments are made in cash, receipts are in cash and are deposited in the company's bank account. Cash balances held in connection with day-to-day activity are referred to as *transaction balances*.

2. *Precaution* — The inflow and outflow of cash is not predictable, although the degree of uncertainty depends upon the particular industry. Just as companies require safety stocks of inventories, they also need some cash in reserve to deal with fluctuations in the inflow and outflow of cash. These reserves are referred to as *precautionary balances*. To the extent that the company is able to borrow on short notice, it requires lower (or no) precautionary balances. As a practical matter, most companies would hold precautionary balances as liquid marketable securities or similar instruments to maximize their income.

3. *Opportunity* — Particularly when economic times are tough, "cash is king". A firm with ready access to cash may be able to take advantage of opportunities as they arise. As with precautionary balances, access to borrowing power, as well as holdings of marketable securities, or other very liquid assets, are alternatives to holding cash.

4. *Finance* — Funds may be accumulated to acquire assets or to retire debt.

5. *Compensating balances* — Depending on the banking arrangements, companies may be required to keep bank balances to provide compensation to their bank for providing services. With the trend towards separating the components of bank service charges, this has become less common. The *Bank Act* provides that compensating balances may not be required under a loan agreement, unless the borrower concurs.

What is Cash?

Most corporate cash is represented by demand deposits at chartered banks, rather than notes or coins. The deposits may have resulted from cheques or cash being deposited, or because the company was granted a loan: the key point is that the corporate cash balance is that against which the company can write cheques.

Marketable securities or other very liquid assets refer to "near cash" or "cash equivalents". *Marketable* means that the securities can be readily sold without disrupting business operations. Other very liquid assets may be redeemable by the holder (for example, mutual funds and some term deposits) even though they are not, strictly speaking, marketable, since they cannot be sold to a third party.

Cash Flow Cycle

Cash is an integral part of most business activity. Inventory is purchased, and eventually paid for in cash. Inventory is combined with goods and services purchased with cash (including employees' salaries and wages), and is converted to something that is sold. For service industries, the inventory may be intangible, but it still results in sales. Those sales create receivables that are eventually converted into cash. Along the way, cash resources may come into the firm by way of loans, other financing, or equity infusions. Cash is disbursed for taxes, interest, and dividends. The notion of a *cash flow cycle* is a powerful and familiar one — with good reason.

The time that it takes cash to flow through the working capital accounts can actually be measured, and the length of the cash flow cycle thereby determined.

The cash flow cycle is defined as the average age of accounts receivable *plus* the average age of inventory *less* the average age of accounts payable.

An important element of the corporate cash manager's job is to control the length of time taken by the cycle. A short cycle is better.

Managing Corporate Cash

Many elements of managing cash involve the same considerations as managing a business. Healthy liquidity is generally the sign of a well-run enterprise. Effective management of day-to-day operating activities both *results* in effective management of cash and banking relationships, and is itself a cause of good cash management.

A successful cash action plan benefits the enterprise in many ways. First, there is renewed emphasis on cash retention. This reduces the costs of obtaining short-term cash, and improves corporate liquidity by establishing a cash cushion. Second, there is a heightened sensitivity to the need for cash and the working capital position. Cash flow and working capital requirements are better understood and eventually used as management tools. Third, there is also an increased focus on the immediate cash consequences of the daily activities of the enterprise. As a result, management will consider the effects on cash and working capital of business decisions. Fourth, the activities of every employee may be related to specific effects on cash. Thus, specific accountabilities and responsibilities may be assigned: measurement of effects on cash and cash flow provide objective quantitative measures. Fifth, the cash action plan provides a common goal for all employees to work towards. Management textbooks emphasize the necessity of enterprises having simple goals on which all staff can focus. The cash action plan broadcasts the notion that all actions can be measured by their effect on cash.

An action plan to manage corporate cash could comprise seven steps:

1. Determine the level of cash.
2. Examine the cash flow cycle.
3. Determine the length of the cycle.
4. Find the bottlenecks that exist in the cash flow cycle.
5. Develop specific action plans to eliminate those bottlenecks.
6. Implement the action plan. Be sure to give individuals very specific responsibility for taking action.
7. Evaluate the results of the action plan (and go back to step 1 or 4).

Cash inflows

The cash action plan starts by looking at the beginning cash balance.

A major goal is to accelerate receipt of cash. Various banking services can be used to this end, depending upon the nature of the business. For example, payments from customers may be accepted directly at bank branches, rather than mailed. This may result in immediate or, depending upon the arrangements, at least, faster credit to the company's account. Occurrences such as mail strikes would thereby have a less disruptive effect. Other bank services such as lock boxes, cash concentration accounts, and mirror accounts all have the effect of making cash receipts available to the enterprise sooner. Talk to your banker.

The process of speeding up on cash inflows requires analyzing cash receipts. Where are payments coming from, and how might they be accelerated to be accessible at one centralized collection point? Centralizing information as to available bank account balances is often the first step in altering the corporate culture to focus more on cash and achieve the advantages set out above.

Numerous techniques are available to better control disbursements. Again, centralized control, or at the very least, centralized information, is often appropriate. Disbursements should be delayed and controlled. If possible, the time that cheques spend in transit should be maximized to increase the "float". Use company credit cards rather than cash advances for travel and entertainment expenses. (Note that the same controls over travel and entertainment expenses, as well as the expense reporting process, should still be required.)

Information Systems

It is essential to have a system with proper financial and management controls. Reports designed to facilitate financial reporting (for example, for the year-end financial statements or for income tax purposes) may be inappropriate for management reporting purposes. Financial reporting is backward-looking. It gives historical information and is often highly summarized. Management reporting is forward-looking and designed to encourage action. It may be quite detailed and specific.

Information must be relevant, otherwise it is useless. To manage cash flows, the enterprise's information systems must generate a cash flow statement. Actually, the "information system" may be manual or manually keyed into a spreadsheet: the important point is to actually report the cash flow information in some way.

Often, management uses the reports that are available, rather than the reports it really needs. A symptom of this is lack of understanding of the reports that are prepared. Consultants often hear: "What does this report mean? What is this information? I don't know how to use it, so why are they sending it to me? Nobody has ever asked what information I need to control cash."

The solution is to ensure that the users are involved in the development of the reports. Often they will learn a lot as well. The format and content of the reports should depend upon how the information is to be used, by whom, and how often. Simply providing "information" is not enough. It may not be relevant, which means that it is not information, it is data.

Budgets

A budget is a financial projection: it is forward-looking and, therefore, an important management planning and control tool. Often, companies have both short- and long-term budgets. The short-term budget is an aid to monitoring and assessing the performance of the business in the current or following fiscal year. Long-term budgets are used to direct the strategy of the enterprise over three to five years.

Comparison of actual to budgeted results provides the management control mechanism. Such performance reports, if prepared promptly, are a powerful management tool — both for the writer and for the recipient. This analysis can be the trigger to carefully consider and resolve problems and opportunities on a timely basis.

The review of cash flows and cash positions should be an integral part of the budgetary process. If cash flows can be anticipated, then management is addressing causality, which is the way to properly take control of cash. The budgetary process is also iterative: interrelationships are studied, factors and assumptions modified, the results examined, and further changes made as necessary. The same process is also appropriate for studying cash flows, again, because of their intimate relationship with all elements of the activity of the enterprise.

The budgetary process also helps ensure accountability as it facilitates reporting by direct responsibility. The effects of individual action can be measured and assessed.

Operations Management

Operations management incorporates the decision-making required for the production of goods and services. "Production" has traditionally been associated with manufacture of goods, using inputs of labour, materials, and overhead. However, service industries also "manufacture" their output, similarly using labour, materials, and overhead. Although their output may not be tangible, principles of sound operations management also apply.

The bulk of the activity of most enterprises is in operations (or production), rather than, for example, marketing or finance.

41

Therefore, the results of operations and improvements to the production process will have the most significant effects on cash and cash flow.

Management of logistics, the flow of goods, and the physical distribution network can free up significant amounts of cash and capital. For example, consider warehousing. Should the product be shipped directly to the retailer, should warehouses across the country be maintained, or should public warehouses be used? In the case of a service, analogous questions apply. How should the service be provided or distributed to the consumer?

Effective management of inventory has been the classic example of freeing up cash while simultaneously forcing the enterprise to focus on its operational efficiency. By eliminating buffer stocks, companies are forced to correct the causes of inefficiencies in their production process.

Working Capital

All cash managers know that their objective is to collect receivables quickly, and pay disbursements slowly. However, there are some relatively subtle ways to do this without irritating customers or suppliers. For example, speeding up all phases of the ordering and billing cycle will not only free up cash, but improve customer service. How long do orders wait before being filled? Why? How long is it before shipments are billed? Why? Is the customer contacted after shipment to ensure that all is satisfactory? If payment is not received, is the customer contacted to see if there is a problem?

In the case of accounts payable, a similar focus on the inventory control, purchase order, and receiving and disbursements function can also be beneficial. Is inventory ordered when it is really needed, or "just in case"? Why? Is the supplier notified promptly of quality, quantity, or damaged inventory problems? Is the receiving process efficient so that shipments received are quickly available for use?

Sundry Cash Disbursements

Fixed assets, income taxes, and similar payments often represent major cash disbursements. Effective control over these payments is ancillary to, and will result from, a well-run business operation.

The timing of major fixed assets purchases should be integrated into the firm's long-term business plans. It is important to separate *operational* decisions (when and what to buy) from *financial* considerations (lease or purchase, how to finance).

Income taxes are a significant component of cash payments. Effective tax planning may defer or reduce tax payments. This may include taking advantage of government assistance schemes and similar incentives. In addition to federal and provincial tax instalments and payments, other disbursements include employee withholding taxes, employment insurance, Canada/Quebec Pension Plan, Goods and Services Tax, other excise taxes, provincial retail sales tax, employer health taxes, capital taxes, workers' compensation premiums, pension plans, and other benefits. Any cash flow budget must consider these often significant and quite "lumpy" payments.

Summary

This chapter presents an overview of considerations that pertain to corporate cash management in Canada. Managing corporate cash is a vital part of ensuring a healthy and viable enterprise.

The broad approach of an action plan is presented, along with typical key concerns, which are developed in more detail in later chapters. This chapter concludes with financial and operations checklists to help evaluate cash management procedures and processes.

Financial Checklist

This cash management checklist covers collections, disbursements, control, and investment. All "No" answers should be followed up, and the "Comments" column should be used for areas that require additional explanation or clarification.

Collections	Yes	No	N/A	Comments
1. Are deposits made on a regular basis, at least daily?				
2. Are deposits made late in the day to include receipts received in that day's mail?				
3. Does the bank provide credit for deposits on the date the deposit is made?				

MANAGING CASH

Collections	Yes	No	N/A	Comments
4. Do employees avoid bank line-ups by dealing electronically or as preferred customers at the branch?				
5. Is mail received throughout the day?				
6. Are appropriate procedures in place to handle remittances from outside Canada?				
7. Are cheques received in the mail deposited the same day?				
8. Do salespeople who pick up cheques turn them in for deposit on the same day?				
9. Are cheques received segregated and deposited immediately, rather than accompany the paper flowing through the accounts receivable department?				
10. Are billings to major customers handled on a priority basis, rather than included with other billings?				

Collections	Yes	No	N/A	Comments
11. Are penalties imposed, or is other appropriate action taken, for customers that do not pay pursuant to billing terms?				
12. Are discount terms not overly generous?				
13. Are invoices processed regularly during the month rather than being held up for month-end?				
14. Are invoices issued within a day of the goods or services being delivered?				
15. Are electronic funds transfer systems being used where appropriate?				
16. Are pre-authorized payments used where appropriate?				

Disbursements	Yes	No	N/A	Comments
1. Are bank accounts consolidated to improve control over costs?				

Disbursements	Yes	No	N/A	Comments
2. Is "positive pay" or are other fraud prevention techniques used to monitor disbursements?				
3. Are disbursement accounts zero-balanced daily to avoid leaving idle balances?				
4. Are bank accounts monitored daily to prevent fraud and monitor disbursements?				
5. Are payments made no earlier than their due date?				
6. Are government remittances, employee deductions, sales deductions, sales tax, etc., being forwarded no earlier than their due date?				
7. Are there special procedures in place for large disbursements to ensure that they are not paid too early?				
8. Are late payment charges avoided by paying invoices on time?				

CANADIAN CASH MANAGEMENT

Disbursements	Yes	No	N/A	Comments
9. Are excessive courier and delivery charges avoided by mailing cheques on time?				
10. Is re-keying of data from bank statements avoided?				
11. Do you know the value of your cheque float?				

Control	Yes	No	N/A	Comments
1. Is the company advised of all cash inflows on the day of receipt?				
2. Are cash receipt reports reviewed on date of receipt?				
3. Does the bank automatically reduce borrowings with funds deposited?				
4. Are daily disbursement reports obtained to allow management to monitor activity and fund as required?				
5. Are daily bank balance reports received and acted on?				

Control	Yes	No	N/A	Comments
6. Do bank reports include all loan and deposit accounts?				
7. Are bank reconciliations prepared at least monthly and reviewed independently of the accounts payable area.				
8. Are cash flow projections updated regularly?				

Investment	Yes	No	N/A	Comments
1. Is the bank service contract negotiated by senior management?				
2. Have bank charges been compared to outside surveys?				
3. Are account balances maintained at appropriate levels given the interest payable on positive balances?				
4. Is there a diary system for maturing investments?				
5. Are automatic note roll-overs in place?				
6. Are maturities matched to cash requirements?				
7. Are cash policies set centrally?				

CHAPTER 4

E-Commerce and E-Payments

Overview

Electronic payments began in Canada as *Electronic Funds Transfer*, or EFT, a means to support automated crediting to or debiting directly from bank accounts for direct credit of payroll, or to collect payments such as insurance premiums and other regular payments. The term *e-commerce* emerged into popular use in the late 1980s, initially to refer to business-to-business electronic transactions. As the Internet has become the ubiquitous mode of communication, much e-commerce is now transacted through the Internet, sometimes using the World Wide Web, sometimes using other modalities.

This chapter reviews various ways of transferring funds other than by the traditional paper-based methods. The Canadian payments system is also reviewed.

Origins of Electronic Payment Transactions

Beginning in the 1960s, financial institutions around the world began to develop the means to convey paperless transactions. In most cases, the intent of these electronic systems was to provide banks the ability to lower operating and infrastructure costs to themselves while offering clients a new service, Electronic Funds Transfer, or EFT.

EFT began in Canada as a means to support electronic crediting to or debiting directly from bank accounts, in support of either direct credit of payroll or to collect for things such as insurance premiums and other regular forms of collections. At the time, many banking organizations were starting to develop relationships with payroll service companies or the payroll departments of larger employers, and saw the opportunity to generate greater margins though an EFT-based service.

The first iteration of the EFT payment systems was based on the exchange of fixed length transactions by tape transported between banks along with the physical cheque exchanges. This tape-based exchange evolved the creation of the CPA005 standard for electronic credits and debits, and was used for nearly 30 years with minor modifications.

Also beginning its primitive existence in the late 60s, the Automated Teller Machine (ATM) or Automated Banking Machine (ABM) came into being, first in the U.S. and then in Canada. These first generation machines were more mechanical than electronic in their operation, but they introduced the idea that money could be conveyed in a manner other than cash or cheque (although they output cash). Credit cards were also emerging in this time frame, and although they were largely paper-based systems, they reinforced again the idea of value transfer through a device or system, namely the plastic card.

None of these new or emerging electronic payment schemes came into being as a stand-alone concept. They resulted from a new service or business approach that demanded a payment process that was more sophisticated than the traditional paper-based schemes of the past. Whether to provide a faster payment, or to lower costs, or to provide a more efficient delivery system or for other reasons, electronic payments evolved from a need that was founded in the changing dynamics of business overall.

Electronic Processes for Business

The term e-commerce emerged into popular use in the late 1980s initially to refer to business-to-business electronic transactions. Since the mid 70s, companies have been developing electronic links with one another to support the purchasing, transporting and invoicing for the supply chain. Many of the larger manufacturers, especially in the automotive sector, had been struggling to lower costs and improve quality to compete on a global scare.

The concept of just-in-time (JIT) logistics was introduced, refined and re-refined to reduce the costs and risks of excessive inventory. At the same time, many JIT companies found that rather than reduce costs, they shifted their costs from the warehouse to the road. Essentially, they had created a logistics management challenge that could only be solved by ensuring as many of the suppliers were using the same JIT techniques as the big manufacturers.

Most of the technical efforts used to provide electronic linkages and management infrastructures were termed Electronic Data

Interchange, or EDI. EDI provided a set of standards, business processes and technologies that allowed companies to link to one another.

In the early days, most of these initiatives were aimed at reducing inventory and accelerating the supply chain, but as these electronic procurement systems and relationships evolved, it became necessary to introduce an electronic payment mechanism to support these initiatives. Suppliers that were JIT for the supply chain wanted to be JIT for payment too. Paper cheques that were paid 60 to 90 days after goods were delivered became a substantial problem for these supply chain participants, many of whom were much smaller and cash flow-challenged.

EDI started with General Motors in 1984 that proclaimed that any of its electronically-linked JIT suppliers could join its EDI-based payment process and receive a guaranteed electronic business payment on a 33-day billing cycle. This initiative, spearheaded by Charles Golden, Corporate Treasurer at the time, was intended to provide a strong incentive to suppliers to become involved with both JIT and its related electronic supply chain improvements.

Electronic commerce (EC) defined

Although the term e-commerce or EC has its roots in the EDI implementations of the late 1980s, the popularization of the Internet has shifted the perception of what the term means. While beginning as a business-to-business reference, with the advent of companies like Amazon.com and eBay, not to mention the impact of the dot-com era, the term has shifted from the idea of corporate exchanges to consumer-oriented processes, that is, online buying of goods and services through Web sites.

This has served only to create confusion and misunderstanding of the meaning of electronic commerce, and resulted in confusion regarding the idea behind e-commerce. Just as the term "food" can mean anything from mealworms to pizza to steak, so too can the term e-commerce cover a lot of different, but equally relevant, meanings.

In its most simple form, e-commerce is about electronically-facilitated transactions. However, it is also about relationships. It is these relationships that define the types of interactions that make up EC. Some relationships are complex and highly interactive involving integration of many organizations and their systems, while others are quite simple and straightforward, like requesting a product of service via a fax or e-mail.

EC involves the application of a number of electronic technologies in combination. Exchanges can be defined on three levels: peer-to-peer, interactive and EDI, or direct data exchange. These are all part of the EC matrix. The distinguishing attributes are:

- Peer-to-peer — Whether using traditional e-mail or real-time exchanges like MSN or AIM, this component of the EC relationship involves interaction between two or more individuals, using computers and telecommunications to create some kind of business activity. The key feature is that humans are involved at both ends of the activity, and are needed to invoke the transaction at one level or another.
- Interactive applications — This set of relationships involves a human at one end of the transaction interacting with a computer or device in a patterned dialogue at the other end. An example of this interaction would be an Automated Banking Machine or Point of Sale terminal, which is completely mechanized in its response, but requires a series of inputs or choices by a human in order to

function. Similarly, a Web site that is set up to take orders and provide automated but intelligent responses would be part of this definition.

- EDI, or other forms of direct data exchange — Electronic Data Interchange (EDI) is the direct, computer-to-computer interchange of structured business documents in a standardized, electronic fashion. This definition can be refined to direct application-to-application exchanges of business transactions. EDI consists of computers from two different organizations sharing and exchanging data with one another, with no human intervention required. This could involve traditional standards for data construction like the ANSI standards, or more modern methodologies such as XML.

Figure 1 — E-Commerce relationships

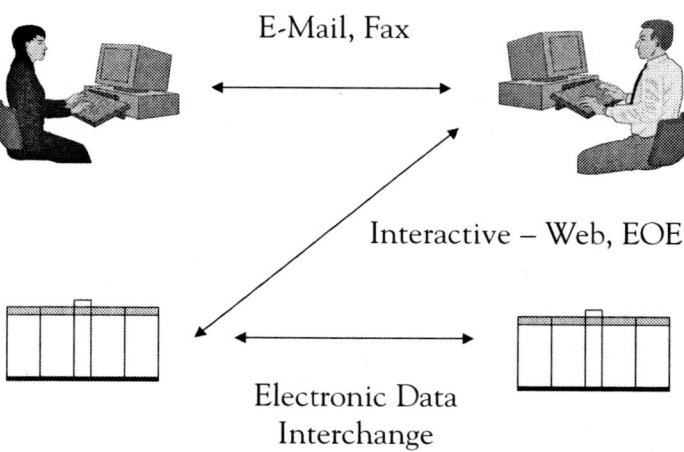

EDI payments process

The use of EDI, and in fact all forms of electronic commerce, is based on a clear intent to accomplish a business objective such as reducing inventory, lowering personnel costs, speeding up access to information, or reducing errors. EDI-based payments are intended to communicate relevant remittance data along with the value transfer, satisfying the recipient's need for reconciling information for the payment. In essence, EDI payments are the equivalent of the cheque and the stub traveling through the payments system in an integrated fashion.

Implementing EDI payments can cause a major change to the culture of any organization — often more than the impact on its systems. Therefore, the factors affecting its use and implementation are often directed towards the minimization or control of the human aspects of the process.

To fully appreciate the business and cultural impacts, the technical process and flows need to be understood.

There are four technology elements to the EDI payments schema:

- Communications facility — either a commercial network provider, bank or Internet;
- A mailbox or similar information storage and forward/retrieval facility (usually part of the communications facility);
- A message structure translator; and
- Applications interface to link the internal system with the outside world.

The Canadian Payments Association (CPA) created rules and standards for the processing of financial EDI transactions in late 1992 under CPA rules E3 and H6. This created a new payment system designed for business-to-business transactions. Under it, all relevant remittance detail can be transferred through the banking system, and it satisfies the needs of both the payment originator and receiver.

Organizations that need to facilitate payments without remittance information can continue to use the EFT system, based on the CPA-005 standard.

The Canadian Payments Environment

The Canadian Payments Association (CPA) is a not-for-profit association that was created in 1980 by an Act of Parliament. The CPA's role, as amended through the *Canadian Payments Act* in 2001, is to:

- establish and operate national systems for the clearing and settlement of payments;
- to facilitate the interaction of its clearing and settlement systems and related arrangements with other systems or arrangements involved in the clearing or settlement of payments; and
- to facilitate the development of new payment methods and technologies.

The CPA is also mandated to address public policy objectives. This requires the Association to promote the efficiency, safety and soundness of the clearing and settlement systems, and to take into account the interests of users and other stakeholders.

There are a number of committees of the CPA to help develop and implement rules that apply to the clearing and settlement of different types of payments between its member financial institutions, ensuring that the system is safe and that payments are exchanged efficiently.

The association also monitors payment system developments and related issues in a global context to ensure the framework for clearing and settlement continues to be relevant and serves the needs of all constituents.

One of the key systems that helps the Canadian payments environment operate in an efficient manner is the Automated Clearing Settlement System.

ACSS overview

The Automated Clearing Settlement System (ACSS), introduced in 1984, is a system that facilitates the accounting and settlement of the majority of payment items in Canada. In 2002, more than 17 million items were exchanged between banks on an average business day's clearing totals.

The term "clearing" refers to a process of exchanging and reconciling individual payment items that result in a transfer of funds between members of the payment system.

The term "settlement" relates to the process of adjusting the different financial positions of each clearing financial institution to reflect the net amounts due to them and from them as a result of the inter-member exchange of payment items. Each direct clearer financial institution in Canada handles the exchange of individual items, but the Bank of Canada is responsible for managing the actual settlement between them.

As of 2003, there are 11 direct clearers in the Canadian payments system, plus the Bank of Canada, making a total of 12 participants. In order to qualify as a direct clearer and gain access to the clearing and settlement system, a financial institution must process at least one half of 1 per cent of the total annual clearing volume (in 2003, this would be 22 million items annually). Direct clearers handle the clearing and settlement of payment items for their own customers, as well as customers that maintain accounts at other financial institutions (known as indirect clearers).

The ACSS is a computer-based information system that tracks both the volume and value of payment items exchanged between direct clearing members of the CPA, and determines the balances due to and from participants. ACSS rules and standards detail the procedures that apply to the exchange, clearing and settlement of items cleared through this system.

The ACSS is used for both paper-based payment items such as cheques and electronic items, including Automated Funds Transfer debits (e.g., pre-authorized debits) and credits (e.g., direct deposits). As of 2002, three-quarters of all payment items exchanged in Canada are electronic-based payments, including EFT, EDI, LVTS, as well as Interac-based shared ATM or Point-of-Sale networks.

How it works

When payment items are exchanged between direct clearers, data is entered into the ACSS to track the total volume and value of items in the particular stream. The direct clearer that is owed money makes these entries. In other words, the delivering direct clearer enters the data for debit streams, and the receiving direct clearer enters the information for credit streams. At the end of the daily exchange process, these entries are used to determine the net positions of the direct clearers.

Direct clearers maintain settlement positions in accounts held at the Bank of Canada. In the morning of each business day, the Bank of Canada adjusts the financial positions of the individual direct clearers by transferring funds among their accounts to reflect the net balances of the previous day's ACSS clearing. In turn, indirect clearers settle the same day with their respective direct clearers through special accounts they maintain with them.

Clearing of electronic payments

The clearing process for electronic payments is more efficient than that of cheques and other paper-based payment items, as there is no requirement to deliver a physical payment item. All processes for the exchange and clearing of electronic payments are fully electronic, although in this situation the ACSS entries reflect national totals rather than regional data.

There are some variations in the procedures and schedules that apply to the various streams of electronic payments, and these are outlined in the CPA's ACSS rules. Within this framework, there may also be some variation in the details of how each direct clearer processes these transactions.

Direct clearers sort and categorize electronic payments by stream and by the direct clearer (and/or indirect clearer) to which they are to be sent. Examples of streams are Automated Funds Transfer (AFT) debits, primarily pre-authorized debits; AFT credits, mainly direct deposits; Electronic Funds Transfer/Point-of-Sale transactions, which track debit card transactions; and bill payments. Most electronic payments are exchanged in bulk between direct clearers over a frame-relay network.

Each direct clearer enters into the ACSS the total volume and value of transactions for which it is owed funds. That is, the direct clearer delivering the transactions will enter the data for debit streams, while the receiving direct clearer will enter the totals for credit streams, such as bill payment remittances. These figures are combined with the totals for all other paper-based payment items to determine the net balances due to and from each direct clearer.

The Bank of Canada then completes the settlement process for each participant's records on the following business morning.

Although the vast majority of the daily transaction volume is cleared through the ACSS (approximately 99 per cent), these transactions represent only about 15 per cent of the total value cleared. A substantial proportion of the total value is cleared via the Large Value Transfer System (LVTS).

Large Value Transaction System (LVTS)

LVTS is the updated electronic wire system introduced by the CPA in February 1999 to facilitate the transfer of irrevocable payments in Canadian dollars across the country in real time. Through LVTS, funds can be transferred between participating financial institutions virtually instantaneously, and the money can thus be credited to the recipient's account on a timely basis. As all LVTS payments are immediately final and irrevocable, the recipient may withdraw the money, invest it or use it to make another payment in full confidence that the incoming payment will not be reversed for any reason.

Any individual payments made in Canada for sums greater than $25 million must be processed via the LVTS, which replaces cheques and any other forms of payment. This means that cash managers and accounts payable commitments will need to consider the implications of forwarding these large value payments through their bank's electronic LVTS-based payment service.

LVTS is unique among payment systems because it is a blend of the two main models used around the world for modern payment systems. It achieves this status because it provides a payment finality that is usually part of a Real Time Gross Settlement (RTGS) system, with the added benefit of lower collateral costs associated with a netting system.

Each payment is final and settlement is assured immediately upon the completion of the individual transaction, even though the actual settlement occurs at the end of the day on the books of the Bank of Canada. The purpose of this approach is to lower the overall (systemic) risk in the payment system. Systemic risk occurs when the inability of one financial institution to meet its settlement obligations could cause other institutions to fail in a domino effect.

In 2002, LVTS was used to clear and settle about $115 billion in Canadian dollar payments each business day, or approximately 85 per cent of the total value moving through the Canadian payments system. Approximately 14,000 LVTS payments are processed each day, with the average value of a transaction in the range of $8 million. LVTS is also particularly suitable for time-sensitive payments of any value.

CPA members that establish and maintain an LVTS settlement account at the Bank of Canada, and provide an acceptable system interface, may participate directly. There are no minimum payment value or volume requirements, although LVTS transactions tend to be for larger amounts.

The Bank of Canada is responsible for monitoring the flow of payments through LVTS, ensuring that participating financial institutions maintain adequate levels of collateral. The CPA administers the daily operations of LVTS, as well as the LVTS rules.

All LVTS payments are final and irrevocable. This means that once a payment is sent, the payer or the financial institution that sent it cannot reverse it. For the recipient, risk is completely eliminated because the payment cannot be withdrawn due to stop payment orders, insufficient funds or forged endorsements. Financial institutions are assured of same-day settlement for LVTS transactions, even in the unlikely event that a participating institution were to fail. This certainty of settlement eliminates systemic risk that could cause a cascade of defaulting financial institutions.

The LVTS has four elements to control and minimize risk:

- The multilateral net debit position of each participant is continually updated based on every payment made in real time by the LVTS system.
- The participants' net debit positions are continuously reviewed against pre-determined ceilings or limits.
- All participants have pledged collateral to the Bank of Canada to cover largest permitted exposure. This ensures settlement for the participants, even if one of them were to default.
- Because of continuous monitoring of exposure, the Bank of Canada can guarantee settlement in the extremely unlikely event that more than one LVTS participant were to fail on the same day during LVTS operating hours.

EDI payment transactions

The transaction format most common for Canadian financial EDI is the ANSI 820. This format permits sufficient detail so that the recipient may reconcile the payment to their accounts receivable records.

This transaction structure, which originated under the American National Standards Institute (ANSI) Accredited Standards Committee (ASC) X12, is incorporated into the CPA regulations as rules E3 and H6.

Transaction flows

To ensure certainty in completing the transaction, multiple acknowledgments are used.

The first acknowledgment (referred to as ANSI designation 997) is a Functional Acknowledgment that may be positive or negative. A positive 997 allows the transaction to proceed to more detailed levels of checking. A negative 997 means that there was something structurally wrong with the message and further action by the originator is required.

If a positive 997 is generated, then an ANSI 824 Application Level Acknowledgment is created — again positive or negative. A negative 824 means that critical data fields are missing or incomplete, or that funds or credit limits are not available. This is somewhat like an electronic NSF notification, albeit before the event has occurred. A positive 824 is an acceptance of the transaction.

Figure 2 — Financial EDI flows

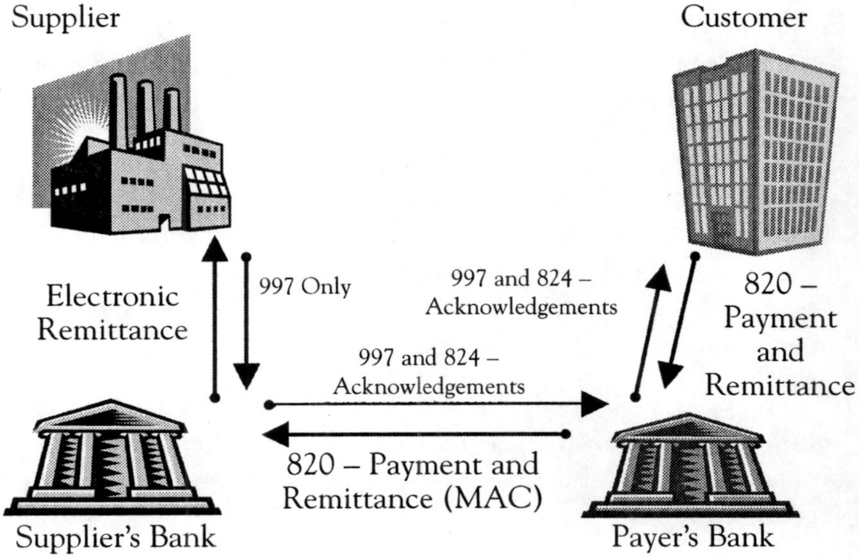

Supplier

Customer

Electronic Remittance

997 Only

997 and 824 – Acknowledgements

997 and 824 – Acknowledgements

820 – Payment and Remittance

820 – Payment and Remittance (MAC)

Supplier's Bank

Payer's Bank

Finally, the 824 is acknowledged by a 997, ensuring that the 824 acknowledgment message arrived back to the originator. This same transfer of acknowledgments is also exchanged between banks if the receiver used a different bank than the originator.

Why use the EDI payment instead of EFT?

Electronic payments from an accounts payable application would ideally provide direct input into an accounts receivable application of another firm. This does not occur with EFT or Wire/LVTS-based transactions because these types of transactions do not convey remittance information in a form that an accounts receivable system can use. If electronic payments do not need to communicate remittance detail, for example, for periodic payments, the use of EFT or LVTS would be appropriate. In other cases, an EDI payment would be preferred.

Accounts payable applications

A payments file is created by the payer's accounts payable system. An EDIT translation program must convert it into an ANSO 820 format. Once it is in that format, it can be encrypted and processed through a security module or process that creates an authentication code.

At this point the transaction is sent and, after the correct acknowledgments are returned, may be considered complete. While there is the possibility that the payee's account may have been closed in the interim, which could still require the transaction to be unwound, this would be very unusual.

The payer's bank will check that the payer is valid, decrypts the transaction if necessary, verifies that the authentication is correct, and confirms that the payee or the payee's financial institution is recognized.

Accounts receivable applications

The seller's accounts receivable contains all the details concerning open invoices. The remittance information must include sufficient detail so that the correct items may be noted as paid. Some applications use mathematical formulae to match the payment to some combination of outstanding invoices to that client.

Other cash application systems require more detail as to each invoice paid and related activities such as adjustments and corrections. EDI is then the best method as it can convey all the necessary information. To process an EDIT payment, a translation program will be required to convert the information to a format recognized by the accounts receivable system.

This may in fact be the same translator used to originate transactions, or it may be a stand-alone translator that automatically dials out to the mailbox on a daily basis, receives the file, sends the necessary acknowledgments, and translates the EDI file into the internal accounts payable format. There is generally no MAC or encryption at this stage because the actual funds transfer has already been handled by the bank.

At this point, the information can be directly applied to the outstanding receivable, marking any of the unpaid items for an "exception report" so that further collection follow-up can be applied. It is more straightforward to receive EDI payments than to send them. The greater amount of effort is by the originator.

EFT

The Canadian EFT transaction standard that is used between banks is commonly referred to as the CPA-005 format. These EFT transactions can be issued in both credit or debit forms and are governed by specific rules for each.

A typical Canadian EFT transaction flows as follows:

- The initiating company creates the payment record in a bank proprietary version of the interbank CPA-005 format. This will include such information as destination, bank and account number, name, amount, value date and a brief description.
- The information is then forwarded to the company's bank (via direct transmission or in smaller volume situations through the bank's cash management service). This is usually done 18 hours or more days prior to the value date to ensure that all end points equal value dating.
- The payer bank will convert the proprietary EFT message into the CPA-005 standard and forward it during the appropriate business day to the receiving bank via transmission though the Automated Funds Transfer system.

Figure 3 — Canadian EFT flows

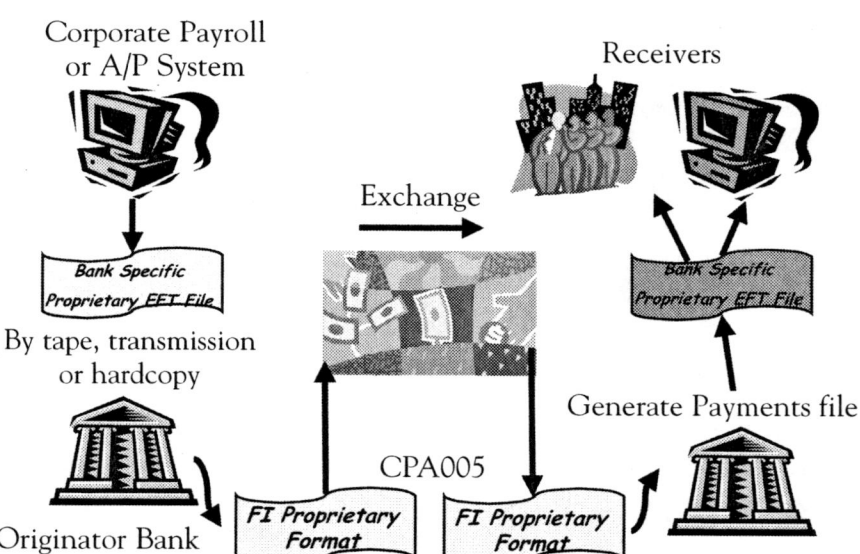

Corporate Payroll or A/P System

Receivers

Exchange

Bank Specific Proprietary EFT File

By tape, transmission or hardcopy

Bank Specific Proprietary EFT File

Generate Payments file

Originator Bank

CPA005

FI Proprietary Format

FI Proprietary Format

- On the value date, all credits or debits are posted and settlement via the ACSS occurs. No acknowledgements for individual events are received.
- The destination client is updated either through a cash management inquiry or via a printed statement of the account.

Emerging Technologies for E-Payments

Smartcards

Smartcards, or stored value cards, are what might be termed "token" cards.

A financial institution will remove money from an account, upon request by the client, and place an equivalent "token" of value on the card. The "real" money remains in the possession of the financial institution until the token is redeemed when the card is used at a later date. In the past, the analogy to this would be the traveler's check.

Smartcard technology has been used in the financial industry for nearly 20 years. Several banks have also experimented with Smartcards for security access application, storing encrypted access codes, and use at the point-of-sale in a stored value application under the brand name of Mondex.

Mondex

Mondex is a specific brand of Smartcard or Stored Value card developed by the National Westminster Bank in the U.K. Its rights were initially sold to Royal Bank in the mid 1990s. The Royal Bank subsequently expanded the participation and ownership rights for the Mondex system to all the major Canadian financial institutions in 1996, and Mondex became the de facto Smartcards standard for Canada. Since that time, the Mondex brand and over-all technology ownership has been purchased by MasterCard International.

Some of the important attributes of the Mondex technology approach are:

- High-grade encryption technology;
- The ability to transfer payments anonymously and directly between individuals as well as with merchants;
- A global brand name.

A pilot project was established in Guelph, Ontario, in early 1997 to determine consumer acceptance of the concept. At its peak, 12,000 Mondex Smartcards were issued and several hundred merchants participated, ranging from parking lots to retail outlets. At the same time, banks in the U.K. were experimenting with their version of Mondex in the city of Swindon.

Both pilot locations have ended. While the banks involved declared that both pilots were successful as a "proof of concept," there have been no further roll-outs or tests.

Debit card

Debit card systems in Canada are now all integrated under the Interac brand. The Canadian debit card concept, which was envisioned as part of the original design of the Interac concept in 1985, began with a pilot project started by the Quebec-based Caisse Desjardins in early 1986, the same year that Interac-shared banking machines services began.

From a technology viewpoint, debit cards are more or less banking machine access cards simply used with a different access device, that is, a swipe device at the point-of-sale. The growth of debit card transactions in Canada has been astonishing, and since 1998, debit cards have become the dominant form of payment next to cash itself. Clearly, consumers are looking at the debit card as their electronic chequebook.

Much of its success is due to cooperation between the major financial institutions and the fact that our financial institutions are national in scope. Part of the reason the United States has not been quite as successful is because they still have regional banking.

The current methodology is that although the merchant has a terminal that connects with the Interac environment through a financial institution, it really has no access to the data. All it gets is an approval or decline. The financial institution then credits the positive responses to the merchant's account at the end of the day.

There are stringent cryptographic requirements to protect the Personal Identification number right at the button level of the key-pad. There is also high-grade cryptography applied in the transaction stream to ensure that client card information is protected.

Telephone banking

There have been telephone-based financial service offerings in the United States since the late 70s. They began to be used in experimental form in Canada in the mid 80s, mainly by the credit union movement.

In the early 90s, Interactive Voice Response (IVR) technologies became more affordable and viable, and telephone-based banking services began to grow into the larger Schedule I banks. This has now turned into a popular service for most Canadian financial institutions.

Most financial institutions now operate their telephone banking front-end, meaning the actual client interface that manages the customer data base and interaction in-house. But many have outsourced the "back-end," which is the data output to the corporate payee. In many cases, this is handled either as a paper output or in the CPA EDI format defined under rule H-6.

Due to its commoditized nature, few banks are looking at telephone banking service and related IVR support systems as a long-term technology platform for the future.

Internet/PC banking services

Although cautious at first, all Canadian financial institutions have now embraced the Internet, especially the Web, as a primary channel for delivering services in the future. Canadian financial institutions were initially concerned about security issues and exposure of client information. However, these concerns have faded as technology has become more robust. The use of Secure Socket Layer (SSL) security, coupled with the prospect of additional layers of security, has mitigated the security concern.

Consumers can now access a full range of banking services through the Web. Businesses now have access to most cash management systems through Web browsers as well.

Electronic bill presentment

There has been a great deal of technology effort expended in the financial community in the area of Electronic Bill Presentment (EBP). The concept behind EBP is to provide a facility for electronic billing distribution for companies like utilities and retailers, or anyone who has to mail out a statement of account.

The motivation for developing this approach is the rapid consumer uptake in PC/Internet/ Telephone banking. Financial institutions believed that consumers who bank electronically would be willing to receive their monthly bills electronically as well. This is supported by the statistic that the growth in pre-authorized debits (direct debits) has grown at the average rate of 16.6 per cent per year for the past four years. POS or debit card transactions have grown at the average rate of 120 per cent per year for the same period.

The counterargument is that consumers do not like to initiate receiving their bills electronically. They prefer to receive them (passively) in the mail. Doubtless, there will be a technological solution to this eventually.

Electronic money

There many emerging schemes that fall into the category of e-money. All of these are focused on the facilitation of payments over the Internet. They all work from the point of view of a "token" of value sent from one computer to another, somewhat like the smart card. The main difference is that rather than loading the tokens of value onto a card device, the value is loaded and stored on a computer hard drive.

No successful e-money programs have emerged yet from this approach. In the short to medium term, credit cards will continue to be dominant for facilitating electronic or Web-based payments.

Micro-payments and mini-payments

Micropayments are extremely low value payments. The basis for this concept is where Web consumers may wish to purchase a single article from an electronic newspaper and pay the component value for this item, perhaps 1/10 of a cent. The reality is that while this is possible, bookkeeping for these types of events is more onerous than the revenue/profit opportunity justifies.

Credit card companies are developing strategies for mini-payments instead, that is, individual items in the unit price range of $0.25 or so. The likely solution will be that minimum accounts balances will be required by the service provider, not by the bank, so one would have to put a $5.00 or $10.00 amount in reserve with the company and draw down on it.

E-payment proxy-based services

Paypal is the most well-known of several e-payment services that have evolved. PayPal acts as a payment intermediary, but is not currently regulated as a financial institution. It provides a service that allows any business or consumer with an e-mail address to send and receive payments online. It uses a secure and fast computer-aided methodology to transport payments through national payment systems of different countries.

Paypal has made arrangements to receive and send payments using the domestic payments infrastructure of each country's banking system. Users must register with Paypal to send money. However, if the recipient has an e-mail address, there does not need to be any pre-registration by receivers. The service is free for payment senders, as all fees and charges are paid by the receivers.

Paypal is an example of the creation of new payment intermediaries that the e-payment process requires. It is different from a token-based payment because it does not purport to provide a transportable, cross-system payment item; rather it takes part of the payment risk and acts as a true intermediary.

Electronic cash management/treasury services

In the late 70s, most of the banks that provided corporate account services developed electronic cash management tools to aid their business banking clients with managing their money better. In doing this, the goal was to generate additional fee revenue, as well as to increase the velocity of cash movement through the system.

All the banks initially developed some form of PC- or terminal-based proprietary system for their business clients to use. Over the past several years, all these proprietary systems have converted to Web-based versions.

E-Payment Standards

Standards are critical for the success of any community with a common interest. They help each participant understand the needs of the others, and provide clarity and objectivity for resolving process issues. Message standards remove any ambiguity in allowing different organizations exchange transactions.

Until 1980 in the Canadian payments environment, most standards were developed by the commercial banks through the Canadian Bankers Association (CBA). Since 1980, with the creation of the CPA, payment system standards have been created and maintained as a common industry group, including banks, Trust Companies, Credit Unions and Caisse Populaires.

There are currently three main groups of standards that are used for Canadian e-payments:

EFT Standards — These are proprietary to the banking system and are created, developed and administrated through the Canadian Payments Association. Standards for EFT (CPA-005) and for other Canadian specific applications have evolved through committee development within the banking community. Most recently, the development of the LVTS standard was undertaken as a specific project, and delivered as a completely new set of transaction standards and processes in 1999.

There are also international standards such as SWIFT (Society for Interbank Financial Telecommunications) that are used by Canadian banks.

EDI Standards — Although adopted into Canadian CPA standards (E3 and H6), the foundation of Canadian EDI Payments standards are based on the ANSI X12 cross-industry standards. The transactions that are facilitated by the EDI structure are as follows:

Figure 4 — EDI transactions

820 - Payment Order (Value and non-value)
821 - Financial Reports
822 - Account Analysis
823 - Lockbox
824 - Application Acknowledgment
827 - Financial Return
829 - Cancel Payment
997 - Functional Acknowledgment

Not all of these standards are ensconced in the CPA rulebook. Many of them are provided as part of the informational services that banks offer and are therefore applied on a proprietary basis by each bank.

In order to use the ANSI X12-based EDI standards, there is generally an interpretive exercise referred to as an Implementation Guide that provides the rules and data descriptions needed to establish an exchange relationship. In many cases, the banks have already developed a template or pro-forma to help this process along. However, the major challenge of establishing an EDI payments program is obtaining the participation of the client or supplier.

New or Emerging Standards — This includes the use of the eXtensible Mark-up Language standard XML. The XML standard is a type of EDI standard, but it differs from the older and more established ANSI approach by providing a methodology to carry both the data and the decoding book in the message. The simplest definition of XML is self-defining documents.

The perceived benefit of XML is that many newer applications carry the XML coding capability as part of their design. The issue or problem is that it still takes quite a bit of set-up, defining and negotiation with a trading partner to establish real connectivity. At present, the use of XML in the payments system is virtually non-existent.

Float Implications for Electronic Payments

"Bank-induced float" occurs when there is a delay between the time a payment is deposited into an account and when value is applied to the account by the bank to the depositor's credit. In the U.S., for instance, it is quite common for a deposit made on the west coast, drawn on a financial institution on the east coast, to have a three- or four-day delay before real value or "good funds" can be applied.

In Canada, there is no bank-induced float under any payment method, be it cheque, EFT or EDI. Instead, in Canada, value is applied immediately. However, from an accounts receivable perspective, the receiving organization still does not know what the funds are for. This is where an EDI transaction can provide value, as the funds and the remittance detail are both delivered together.

There is, however, a mail float in Canada. This term refers to the period of time from when the stamped envelope is put into the postal system to the time the recipient opens the envelope and deposits the payment item.

In the past, payment terms tended to be based upon when a cheque was posted. It is becoming more common to specify when payment must be received, which creates a motivation to use more effective payment instruments such as EDI. In the event, EFT and EDI payments can offset the costs of mail float and missed discounts by facilitating quicker transactions.

Ironically, the LVTS system may induce a one day float, depending on the timing of the transaction. Because the originating bank has to provide collateral to offset the transaction risk, transactions may be held overnight before final processing to the recipient.

Procurement cards

The procurement card is a relatively recent phenomenon that uses a consumer-based credit card and its support infrastructure, but focuses on supporting business-purchasing activities. Procurement cards work best for low-dollar, high-volume activities, like buying office supplies.

In many organizations, low-value, high-volume purchases can account for as much as 70 per cent of total transaction volumes, but less than 10 per cent of total money spent. Often, the administration costs of these activities can exceed the prices of the actual purchases. In these cases, traditional business purchasing techniques such as EDI do not fit well because of the effort needed to administer the ordering process and enroll the supplier. By charging the items to a procurement card, many costly manual procedures disappear or are streamlined.

The key values of such a card are to:

- Increase efficiency by reducing the paperwork required to manage small value transactions;
- Reduce inventory and space requirements by acquiring low value commodity products as they are needed;
- Lower the overall cost per transaction;
- Exercise more control over purchasing and payables through improved tracking of the financial activity;
- Improve supplier relations by using a tool which has almost immediate payment (as opposed to the supplier waiting 30 plus days for an invoicing cycle);
- Obtain supplier discounts where volume can be established.

All major credit card issuers offer procurement card programs and have significant success in marketing them to medium- to large-sized firms. Small enterprises are not as likely to use the procurement card because of their inherently low overhead costs.

Balance and transaction reporting

As organizations become increasingly global in their operations, there is a need to understand their balance sheet on a total company basis. Even in countries such as Canada that have national banking systems, there can be significant complexities in arranging for consolidated transaction and balance reporting.

ANSI standard 821 can accommodate balance and transaction reporting, and supply detail in a standardized format. This means that a company can receive the information from two or more banks in the same format. This then permits the company to organize the information from a variety of banks and compare it in a meaningful way.

Generally, if an organization uses only one or perhaps two banks, it is usually more effective to use the cash management service their bank offers. If an organization deals with multiple banks, or is consolidating information from banks in the United States, Canada and elsewhere, then there may be merit in using the 821.

E-Payments Outside of Canada

The United States

While U.S. cheques can be drawn on Canadian banks, many Canadian firms operate accounts at a U.S.-based bank to overcome float delays and ease the management of foreign exchange. As well, in many cases, cross-border electronic payments can be facilitated through SWIFT-based transfers or bilateral arrangements between a U.S. and Canadian bank. Typically, however, cross-border electronic payments are awkward, difficult and often expensive for both the payer and the receiver.

There has been a great deal of work over the past decade to develop a more compatible exchange process between Canada and the U.S., leading to the creation of the Cross Border Payment (CBP) transaction in the U.S. This transaction provides for the insertion of an EFT or single-remittance segment EDI into or out of the U.S. Automated Clearing House (ACH) system.

Alternatively, many of the larger Canadian commercial banks have established full-blown EDI relationships with a partner bank in the U.S. to facilitate a cross-border transaction via a correspondent relationship. This does not resolve the issue of the multitude of banks in the U.S. that still remain unable to receive or distribute remittance details, and are forced to send an EFT and transport the remittance detail to the receiver in another fashion.

Conclusion

E-payments are now the dominant form of exchange in Canada — whether using EFT, EDI, LVTS methods. To maximize the value obtained from using e-payments, organizations need to focus on automating the integration between the banking system and their accounting systems. Successful organizations have integrated and automated links to minimize manual intervention. This improves the speed, accuracy and efficiency of their receipts and payment processes.

CHAPTER 5

Credit and Collection

Overview

Managing working capital is one of the most important responsibilities of the financial manager. Outflows of cash are often relatively well controlled. Cash inflows — such as bank borrowings and collection of accounts receivable — are inherently less controllable. Nonetheless, accounts receivable is usually a major component of working capital, so there can be significant financial benefits if it is well controlled. In addition, a thorough understanding of accounts receivable can lead to improvements in marketing, customer service, and other areas.

Basis for Credit

When credit is granted, two fundamental assumptions are made: *confidence* and *futurity*.

The party that extends the credit must have *confidence* that the other party will be both willing and able to repay the obligation when it comes due. **Willingness** depends upon the character of the debtor. **Ability** to pay depends upon the financial strength and capability of the debtor. This may be influenced by external factors such as the state of the economy, the business environment, and so on.

Futurity refers to the notion that the future is never certain. (Some people find it hard enough to predict the past.) Consequently, every potential credit transaction requires an answer to the question: is this transaction worth the risk of possible loss? In contemporary corporate finance terms, the question would be whether there is a sufficiently high reward to risk ratio to make the transaction worthwhile.

Credit as a Strategic Tool

Credit policy can be used positively, as a strategic tool. A significant example of this is the use of credit to promote sales: credit may be as important as delivery dates, price or quality in securing an order. Examples of credit policy used strategically are:

- *Marketing* — Credit can be a mechanism to expand into new territories, new product lines, or otherwise endeavour to obtain a competitive edge.
- *Seasonality* — Credit can help smooth out what would otherwise be seasonal variations in sales, for example, in the farm equipment or fashion industries.

- *Improves purchasing power* — The availability of credit may improve the ability of the purchaser to buy goods and services (although, perhaps only temporarily).

Abuse of Credit

Credit can be abused. This can occur in many different ways, and may involve the following:

- *Extravagance* — It may be too tempting to improve the lifestyle of a business — or consumer — if someone else's money is involved.
- *Speculation* — The temptation to take an undue amount of risk may be too strong.
- *Overexpansion* — Credit extended unwisely and taken inappropriately has led to the collapse of many businesses.
- *Overtrading* — From the perspective of the credit grantor, too much capital tied up in accounts receivable can result in excessive interest expense or even bad debt write-offs.
- *Fraud* — Despite rapid communications, good information availability, and state-of-the-art computerization, it can be relatively easy to defraud an unsuspecting grantor of credit.

Credit Policy

Credit has a central role in the profitability and solvency of an organization. Credit is also a major marketing tool and affects many other corporate functions. Consequently, every enterprise should have a credit policy.

Creating a credit policy

There are three steps to be taken in formulating a credit policy:

Objectives of company in areas of sales, profits, marketing strategy and product development must be determined and integrated with the objectives of the credit function.

The second step is to assess the *internal and external influences*. Some of the influencing factors would be industry conditions, competitive influences, the company's capital and financial condition and the compatibility factor with other departments. Minor influences might include availability of credit information and industry terms of sale.

The third factor is *tactics,* which involves deciding what courses of action will result in the achievement of the goals within the constraints of the industry conditions and general economic factors.

Credit policies may be classified as *lenient* or *restrictive*. Degrees of each will often exist within company divisions or units, depending upon profit margins and competitive conditions.

A lenient policy may accept larger risks or permit larger amounts of credit. A lenient policy is common in heavy competition, highly profitable industries or in new territory selling situations. Little or no credit investigation is made into well-known or well-rated concerns and marginal accounts receive only a cursory investigation, perhaps a simple reference check or bank report.

A restrictive policy may be called for if there is little or no competition, a low profit margin, low sales volume, if the product is custom-made or if the company has a poor cash position. As well, if demand for the product or service is high, selective culling of accounts may build profits.

A restrictive credit policy may be offset with a more lenient collection policy. The reverse is also true. A lenient credit policy can be countered with an aggressive collection policy. This is what happens in industries such as trucking, or the courier business. Unfortunately, too many companies have lenient credit and lenient collection policies, the results of which can be disastrous in terms of bad debts.

Developing and communicating a credit policy

In most companies, the responsibility for establishing the parameters of a credit and collection policy rest with the Chief Operating Officer or the Chief Financial Officer. The responsibility for administering the policy will rest with the Credit Manager. The policy is different from the procedures used to carry out the policy. A policy will apply to general, common situations that extend over long periods of time. In a sense, the credit policy is the link between the goals and the specific directives used to achieve the goals. In this respect, a policy may contain the actual credit department goals in areas such as assistance to other departments, for example, sales. Safeguarding major investments and goals of marketing may also be included. A sample of a generic credit policy follows this section.

Once formulated, the credit policy should be communicated to all areas of the company: accounting, sales, production and marketing departments. A précis of the policy may be provided to all customers in the form of a "welcome" letter to new accounts and follow-up letters to existing accounts.

Example of a credit policy

Credit Policy

Subject
Accounts Receivable — Credit & Collections.

Objective
To establish guidelines for the extension of credit, recognizing the importance of the credit function in protecting the Company's investment in receivables while, at the same time, not hindering the development of profitable sales.

Applicability
Applies to all divisions and subsidiary companies of _____ .

Responsibility
The General Manager responsible for each operating unit is responsible for the effective utilization of the credit and collection function.

Every company division is responsible for its own written accounts receivable *procedures* which must conform to this policy. Where extraordinary circumstances warrant deviation, these must be specifically covered by the company in writing and approved by the Corporate Vice-President, Finance.

General Policies
All credit granting and collection procedures will be approved by the Credit Manager.

Credit Approval
Existing customers as well as prospective customer with whom we anticipate doing busi-

ness, must be investigated for the purpose of establishing, reconfirming, modifying and monitoring their credit standing and limitations. The degree of investigation will be dictated by the anticipated value of the order or account, risk involved, and profitability of the sale. For any open lines of credit in excess of $50,000, a financial statement of the customer must be obtained.

The Division Credit Manager is responsible for keeping the Sales Department informed of receivable balances and credit limits for each customer, usually through monthly agings and advice on selected accounts. A copy of all credit department correspondence will be routed to the General Sales Manager.

A credit application will be completed for every new customer. As well, a customer update request will be sent to every customer at least once per year to ensure that information on ownership and financial results are current.

Credit Verification — Many sources of credit information are available such as credit reference books, credit reporting agencies, banks, other vendors. The Credit Manager shall implement a program using the most appropriate sources available, maximizing outside services and information to the fullest degree. Credit limits should be established for both new and existing customers. Systems must also be in place to ensure complete and up-to-date information on existing customers.

Terms of Sale

The Company's terms of sale are net 30 days. Other terms require prior approval from the General Credit Manager. Alternatives to open accounts such as deposits will be used for those customers unable to meet our standards. The responsibility for informing the customers of the terms and conditions of sale rests primarily with the sales department.

Collections

One of the prime requisites for effective collection effort is prompt and accurate billing. Controls shall be established and enforced by the Credit/Financial Manager to ensure compliance. The invoice is the first line of collection. Terms and conditions of sale will be prominently displayed on all invoices.

Complaints regarding billing must be acknowledged promptly and resolved within a reasonable time. Many customers will withhold payment of an entire invoice pending receipt of an adjustment, which may represent only a fraction of the invoice.

Collection effort, to be effective, must be consistent, usually through the use of letters, telephone contacts, sales department contacts and personal visits, depending on the circumstances and amount of the billing involved. Appropriate procedures may vary from division to division, the General Credit Manager will have the responsibility to ensure that proper training and procedures are in effect.

When the situation warrants, and after other collection efforts have been exhausted, uncollected accounts should be referred to the appropriate collection agency, generally when the account reaches 75 days past due.

Although operating management with the aid of salespeople, may be consulted and used to assist in the collection effort, the primary responsibility for collections rests with the Division Credit Manager.

Accounts Receivable

1. *Records and Agings.* Individual records for each customer will be maintained. The monthly aging of receivables information should reflect the following:

(a) Name of account;

(b) Total amount due;

(c) Aged balances:

Current
31 – 60
61 – 90
91 – 120
121 – 1 year
Over 1 year;

2. *Comments — Past Due Accounts.* Accompanying the aging should be reports providing comments and additional data on

specific accounts over $10,000 over 60 days old, including specific actions that have been and will be taken and the probability of collection.

3. *Uncollectables.* Accounts that are uncollectable should be written off when reasonable collection means have been exhausted. The Credit Manager must ensure that all write-offs are approved by the appropriate operating manager. Although charged to the appropriate Reserve For Uncollectable Accounts, active collection must be continued until the account is collected or determined to be uncollectable owing to bankruptcy, out of business without further recourse, or similar reason. Proof of uncollectability, usually a collection agency report, or bankruptcy proceedings should be obtained and maintained in the customer file to support such write-offs.

4. *Recoveries.* Any recovery of accounts previously written off must be credited to the same reserve account charged with the uncollectable.

Insolvency

A copy of all correspondence regarding matters of insolvency or business failure will be routed to the General Credit Manager, who will be responsible for directing the measures appropriate to assuring the Company's continuing involvement in all meetings relating to our position as a creditor.

Opening Credit Accounts

Applications and forms

Building a credit system is based upon sound principles, first and foremost of which is a strong information system. This usually begins with the *credit application.*

The credit application should be designed to encompass credit policies and objectives, as well as industry practices. Beginning with the legal name of the business, any trade styles used, physical address, names of owners/principals/officers, the home addresses of the principals and so on, the application becomes a verifiable document. Verification will depend upon the time needed to make the analysis, amount of the credit line, and degree of difficulty obtaining information.

The application should be completely filled out and signed by an appropriate person within the prospective company.

Role of the sales representative

The sales representative is usually the first contact with a new customer can be of immense aid in ensuring that the customer gets started on the right foot. Many companies use a Sales Report so that any information the representative may have about the account will be included in the analysis. This information might include:

- Names of other suppliers;
- Type of products manufactured/wholesaled or service performed;
- Opinion of facilities, general condition of plant;
- Opinion of management;

- In new businesses, an opinion as to the qualifications of principals; and
- Economic conditions in the sales territory.

The amount of information and degree of completeness will, of course, be commensurate with both the risks and the opportunities for future business. If the sale is a one-time purchase, the long-term solvency of the account is secondary to the short-term liquidity. In any case, it is important to take advantage of the knowledge gathered by the sales representative and to involve them in the data collection process.

Updating information

Once accounts are opened, most companies rely only on hearsay or rumours to keep up-to-date on changes within existing customers. Unfortunately, the bankruptcy files are full of out-of-business companies that paid their bills promptly right up to the date of filing. Even though an account has been on the books for years, the vigilant credit professional keeps a close watch to note even apparently small changes such as a minor change in the name of the customer.

Other companies send credit update requests to customers on a regular basis. In most instances, only basic information is requested, for example, change of management, bank, etc. If the name of the party responsible for the account was not on the original application, this is a good time to request that person's name. This is a key collection requirement.

Extending Credit

Information requirements

The extension of credit will be guided by several factors, including amount and frequency of orders, industry conditions and external factors in such areas as marketing strategies.

The credit information to be collected, in addition to the credit application, can be varied and possibly time-consuming. Company sales personnel, interviews with customers by telephone or in person, banks and other financial institutions, trade references, public records, and credit agencies such as Dun & Bradstreet are the most common. On the basis of the evaluation, credit lines or limits can be established in accordance with pre-set guidelines. Alternatives to regular open-account terms should also be in place. If, for instance, 30-day terms appear to be unacceptable for a particular account, would an advance deposit make the order more acceptable?

The analysis, following the credit investigation, will again be varied according to the company conditions, but generally will follow these areas:

- Organization of business;
- Length of time in business;
- History of business;
- History of principals;
- Operation of business;
- Financial information;
- Payment history;
- Banking sources and relationships; and
- Industry and economic conditions.

Organization of business

The three major types of businesses in Canada must be understood in order to identify the extent of responsibility of the owners or shareholders.

1. *Sole Proprietorship* — The sole proprietorship is a business owned by one person. This type of operation is common in the smaller business and is easily formed. The owner of such a business has both personal and business assets at stake and is personally liable for all indebtedness.

   There are significant disadvantages to dealing with proprietorships. As the business failure statistics indicate, one person often cannot conduct efficiently all important facets of a complex business as it grows. In the event of death or illness, a creditor may have to wait long periods for payment of bills. Heirs seldom run the business as successfully as the founder. Finally, the most important reason is simply control. A sole owner has no one to answer to and can divert funds for any purpose.

2. *Partnerships* — A partnership is an association of two or more persons to carry on as co-owners, much the same as a proprietorship. The legal status of partnerships is based upon common law and statute which pictures the organization as an aggregate of individuals who can be sued, for instance, in the names of the partners. In a *general partnership,* each partner has unlimited liability to creditors. In a *limited partnership,* limited partners are liable only to the extent of their investment, but there must be one or more general partners. A partnership composed of active businesspeople will tend toward a more flexible and competent management than a proprietorship, if the partners have diversified abilities and experience. The disadvantages of dealing with this type of business from a creditor's point of view lie

mainly in the control and stability areas. Dissension and friction among the partners often seriously retard business progress. The stability and continuity of a partnership is uncertain, for instance, upon a partner's death, insolvency, lunacy or withdrawal. For these reasons, financing is often difficult to obtain in large amounts.

3. *Corporations* — A corporation is an artificial body created by law which empowers the organization to act in many respects as an individual. A corporation stands on its own and has a perpetual life so that the death or withdrawal of a shareholder does not affect the business stability or continuity. Unlike proprietorships and partnerships, shareholders and managers of a corporation are not liable for its debts. The shareholders may lose whatever investment was made in the shares of the company, but they will not be called upon to meet the debts in the event of the assets becoming insufficient. Because of the limited liability, this has become the most common type of ownership in Canada for all but the smallest business.

Other forms of business ownership such as cooperative and joint ventures are less frequent but should be recognized during the credit analysis.

Cooperatives are found in the farming, marketing and financial (credit unions or caisses populaires) industries. In many respects, they are similar to corporations, the capital being supplied by members who buy shares. Surplus earnings may be distributed to members by way of dividends or immediate savings on purchases.

Joint ventures are associations of two or more business organizations formed to carry out a single business transaction. The construction field frequently has these types of entities. The legal responsibility is generally similar to a partnership.

In assessing the creditworthiness of a customer or prospective customer, the type of business ownership is a key factor. When possible, every effort should also be made to determine if there is a parent-subsidiary relationship, or affiliated companies involved in the day-to-day affairs of the customer.

Length of time in business

The length of time in business, from a credit standpoint, refers to the length of time the owner has been in control of the business. The first six years of a business' life is a critical period. The testing of the company's management, marketing and personnel occurs during this period. Interestingly, the first year of a business is very low in failures, probably because the company has not devoured its capital, nor run out of available suppliers. Some companies will not deal with businesses which have been in existence for one year or less, although such a policy is normally too restrictive.

New businesses

The assessment of a new business should fully cover two important areas:

1. Amount of starting capital;
2. Source of the starting capital —
   The usual sources of capital include:
   - Savings;
   - Loans from relatives or banks;
   - Inheritance;
   - Sale of another business; and
   - Sale or mortgage of property.

The source and amount of starting capital is an excellent indicator of the owner's commitment level, as well as providing financial information.

Nature and operation of business

What a company does, how it does it, and who it competes against are the basic ingredients of a credit analysis. In analyzing a company's financial condition, the line of business determines, for example, whether an accounts receivable figure is too high, too low or about average for the industry. Does management have experience in the line of business? It is difficult to say without knowing the line.

The line of business can often be determined by knowing the company's name, however, this can easily be wrong or misleading. The line of business can commonly be determined from the credit application or salesperson's report. Commercial credit reports also provide the SIC (Standard Industrial Classification).

Retailers

- Most retail lines are very competitive. Some lines are dominated by large chains that control pricing.
- The buying process is most important. Management must be experienced or employ experienced personnel.
- Gross profits are higher than wholesalers.
- In the grocery business and certain other retail businesses, the stores control the allocation of shelf space so that manufacturers have relatively little power.

Wholesalers

- Profit margins are usually low.
- Competition is not that great in most lines and few industries are dominated by large firms.
- There is usually only a small investment in fixed assets.

Manufacturers

- As principal costs are labour and materials, working capital is a key influencer in the credit decision.
- Long-term debt may be high to finance working capital and fixed assets.
- Extent of competition varies widely; influences are difficult to determine.

Transportation

- Profits are very low and the industry is highly competitive.
- Labour and fuel are the major costs.
- Very little inventory carried.

Seasonality

Many lines are more affected by seasonal characteristics, for example, farm equipment, fashion industries and department stores. It is important to determine what the major selling season is and what effect it has on cash position. In the fashion industry, for instance, inventory build-up in the spring for the fall lines will mean low cash positions and very often operating losses for the period. The nature of the product and the diversity of products within a company's lines should also be assessed.

Types of customers and number of accounts

The quality and number of accounts a prospective customer has are important. A company's fate may be in the hands of one or two major customers, the loss of which may cause a rapid deterioration and eventual failure. Alternatively, selling to a large number of clients may cause a load on the staff, facilities and systems to handle the volume.

Credit information

Bank references

Checking bank references is a common practice in Canada. The two means of obtaining banking reference information are to use your own bank or to deal directly with the prospective customer's bank. Your customer's banking relations are in many cases his or her most important financial relationship. Banks are intimately involved with the activities of their accounts when financing is involved. A simple switch in banking source is a major change in most cases, important enough that several companies' procedures call for immediate reassessment of a customer's credit lines when a bank is changed. The credit manager must realize, however, that the banker's relationship is different from the unsecured creditor and there may be instances, particularly when the collateral may be *your goods*, that the bank's interests may be at odds with these suppliers.

When banking sources are checked, it is important that the information be as factual as possible. Whether the banking relationship is described as "satisfactory for normal commitments" or "considered satisfactory for requirements" is less important than factual information that supports the whole story of the business.

Generally, the information requested should consist of all or part of the following:

- How long the bank has had the account;
- Borrowing or non-borrowing account;
- Security on loans;
- Fluctuations in loans; and
- Fluctuations in cash balances.

Credit agencies

Reports from credit agencies can be a useful source of information. In Canada, reports are available from D&B Canada (*www.dnb.ca*), Equifax Canada Inc.(*www.equifax.com/EFX_Canada*) and Canadian Credit Reporting Ltd (*www.canadiancredit.com*).

All agencies provide payment history for various suppliers, in addition to financial information, and other useful information such as claims, banking information and existing credit granted. The credit agencies also provide a record of recent enquiries, as well as a proprietary credit score to rate creditworthiness of the account.

Some industries and associations also provide credit reports to members, consisting mainly of trade information and varying amounts of other information. The quality and scope of the information varies, but the dates can be useful since it is industry-specific.

Public record and corporate information

If an outside agency is not used as a source of information, the credit investigation should also include the means to check sources of corporate information. A great deal of information is in the public records. Writs, judgments, real estate transactions, registered debt, financing statements and mortgages are all available. The following is a list of sources for provincial and federal corporations. This information will include incorporation details, correct legal name, and names of shareholders of record. The same offices in Ontario also house all registrations under the *Personal Property Security Act*, an invaluable source for investigating a company's registered debt. Fees vary by jurisdiction.

Federal: Corporations Canada
9th Floor, Jean Edmonds Towers South
365 Laurier Avenue West
Ottawa, Ontario
K1A 0C8
Tel: (866) 333-5556
www.strategis.ic.gc.ca

Alberta: Corporate Registry, Companies Branch
8th Floor North, 10365 97th Street
Edmonton, Alberta
T5J 3W7
Tel: (403) 427-2311
www.gov.ab.ca/gs/services/cpns/index.cfm

British Columbia: Registrar of Companies
940 Blanshard Street
Victoria, British Columbia
V8W 3E6
Tel: (604) 387-4471

Manitoba: Corporations Branch
405 Broadway, 10th Floor,
Woodsworth Bldg.
Winnipeg, Manitoba
R3C 2L6
Tel: (204) 994-2500
www.gov.mb.ca

New Brunswick: Department of Justice, Corporate
Services Division
P.O. Box 6000
Fredericton, New Brunswick
E3B 5H1
Tel: (506) 453-2703

Newfoundland: Department of Consumer and
Commercial Affairs
Atlantic Place, 5th Floor, Water St.
St. John's, Newfoundland
A1C 5T7
Tel: (709) 737-2781
www.gov.nf.ca/gsl/cca

Nova Scotia: Department of the Attorney General
Registryof Joint Stock Companies
P.O. Box 1529
Halifax, Nova Scotia
B3J 2Y4
Tel: (902) 424-7770
www.gov.ns.ca/snsmr/rjsc

Ontario: Minister of Consumer & Business
Services
Companies Branch
393 University Avenue
Toronto, Ontario
M7A 2H6
Tel: (416) 963-0552
www.cbs.gov.on.ca

P.E.I.:   Department of Justice
Corporations Division
P.O. Box 2000
Charlottetown, Prince Edward Island
C1A 7N8
Tel: (902) 643-5253

Quebec:	Inspecteur General des Institutions Financieres Companies Service 800, Place d'Youville Quebec, Quebec G1R 4Y5 Tel: (418) 643-3625 *www.revenu.gouv.gc.ca*
Saskatchewan:	Registrar of Companies 2121 Saskatchewan Drive, 3rd Floor Regina, Saskatchewan S4P 3V7 Tel: (306) 565-2962

Internet

Many companies have a Web site setting out their history, management, business and other information. Often they provide links to press releases and financial statements. Spending a few minutes browsing through sites can be a valuable source of information.

Use a reliable search engine to look for other references to the company on the internet. This can provide information such as positive or negative press reports and lawsuits.

Direct dealings with customer

Although common sense suggests the desirability of direct contact with the customer, this is often only done at the end of the collection process. Personal calls to customers eliminate any confusion that correspondence might cause. Personal calls build customer goodwill, make it easier to request financial information directly, and give the credit manager the opportunity to see the facilities and the condition of the equipment.

Credit department records

Beginning with credit applications, the professional credit department maintains credit files on each customer. Depending on the complexity of the credit operation, the variations can range from computerized files on each account, tickler or accordion files. Standardized forms are helpful for credit applications, sales department information, shipping records, payment history (particularly if the information on payment history is not permanently stored in a computer system). Other forms should be prepared in advance, such as personal guarantee forms. It has been said that documentation is the heart and soul of collection work, the same can be said for credit files.

Management history

Analyzing the character and management capacity of the principals is important, but often neglected. While current financial information is difficult to gather, it is reasonably easy to analyze. Historical information, on the other hand, is both difficult to obtain *and* difficult to analyze; however, there may be no better prediction of the future than the lessons of the past.

Character

Willingness and ability is shown by the past record. The credit analyst should look for the following:

- Past history of lawsuits or bankruptcy/business failure;
- Past experience in line of business;
- Management experience;
- Age;
- General reputation in community; and
- Other business interests.

Financial statement analysis

Financial statements are not readily supplied by private companies in Canada. In the last decade, however, more and more credit policies include a requirement for financial statement information at some level of credit exposure. A financial institution rarely provides credit lines of any significance without complete and full disclosure. The professional credit department should be guided by the same principles.

The various ratios used in financial statement analysis are discussed in Chapter 7 of *Canadian Treasury Management.* In addition to horizontal, vertical and ratio analysis, the credit analyst should be particularly attentive to working capital.

Working capital analysis

Working capital, the excess of current assets over current liabilities, is used to finance the current operations of a business. The amount of working capital a company has and the consituents of its assets and liabilities, relates directly to the company's ability to pay its bills. Insufficient working capital is a major cause of failure.

Working capital analysis reveals what funds are available from one period to the next and what application has been made of the funds; for example, a dividend policy may deplete the working funds or permit a healthy increase in net worth if earnings are retained.

Other questions that arise are:

- Has new financing been used to strengthen working capital or finance an expansion of fixed assets?
- Have earnings been sufficient to provide for growth and increased sales volume?

Credit assessment without financial information

While financial information is one of the best ways to evaluate a company's creditworthiness, only rarely will a supplier have such a restrictive credit policy that a lack of financial information prevents opening an open account. Credit strength is easily demonstrated without providing a financial statement (a major reason why managers decline to provide them). If a business' payment record is prompt, if it doesn't borrow or have registered debt, if management seems experienced, a financial statement may not be required.

Many times, it is fairly easy to gauge a company's size from the sales levels or number of employees. Combined with a representative trade supplier survey and a good factual bank reference, a good estimate of financial position can be made.

Setting Credit Limits

The credit limit is the maximum amount of credit a company will extend to a customer. Further shipments will be stopped when the limit is exceeded until payments are made. The disadvantages of using credit limits are:

- If the method of setting the limit is faulty, too much credit can be extended.
- The alternative is also true: business could be turned away unnecessarily.

The advantages of credit limits lie in the speed of order processing. Orders can be approved automatically, saving time and paper work. Orders are shipped faster and often costs are decreased.

Methods

There are several methods of setting credit limits. Depending upon the classification system utilized, the most common of which are the following or some derivation of the following:

- *Requirements limit,* that is, no limit— applicable to the largest clients or government accounts.
- *Usual requirements limit* — normal requirements are determined by past experience or normal industry practices.
- *Size of order* — an order limit can be established easily beyond which approval is required. This might not be desirable in a multi-branch ordering situation as credit exposure can increase quickly.

Setting monetary limits is a source of difficulty for many credit professionals. Various formulas have been devised, including the following:

- *Financial statement method* — based on the results of an analysis of financial statements, a credit limit of 5 per cent to 10 per cent of net worth or working capital can be set. Other factors such as economic conditions, marketing strategy can enter into the decision. This method would be used with a long-term customer or upon entering a relationship of more than a single order.
- *Credit agency ratings* — a simple method that sets limits on the basis of a credit rating. For example, a poor rating could receive a limit of $3,000, while a AAA or government could receive a requirements limit. While the credit rating system is based upon careful and totally objective investigation, the absence of ratings in many cases will require that a "manual" system of setting limits on the ratings be also set up.

Whatever the method, its use must be tempered by practical considerations. What the competition does often has the greatest influence. If a competitor is extending credit up to $50,000, comparable limits may have to be set to avoid losing a customer. Obviously, the size and financial situation of your company has a great influence. A financially strong company can use this strength to great advantage. When combined with good collection policies, the risk is reduced; however, the reverse is also true.

Collection Practices

Some credit departments mistakenly separate the functions of credit from collection. There is no doubt that collection practices need to conform to the overall credit policies and circumstances. Collection approaches need to recognize product and customer characteristics, competitive factors, profit margins as well as economic conditions that exist, and yet the vast majority of Canadian companies treat the collection function haphazardly and without a strategy. Simply using a variety of collection techniques without thought to the ramifications may collect the accounts, but with the loss of the customer.

A working collection policy is the key to improving the efficiency of the function. The primary responsibility of the credit manager is to manage the risk, thus increasing sales. The second responsibility is to administer the systematic, steady progression of collection steps, which can only be accomplished with well-defined policies and procedures.

Past due charges

Many sellers charge — or attempt to levy — customers a past due charge. This rate is usually set by industry standards, when in fact the charge should be set to exceed the approximate cost of capital.

In the real world, however, there are problems with past due charges. The primary difficulty is the legal collectability of the charges. Should the account become uncollectable, the past due charges may not be collectable since most credit applications are not contracts. Another difficulty is that the customer may not accept the change and simply refuse to pay.

Collection responsibilities

While the vast majority of companies use the same personnel who made the credit decision for the collection process, there is an increasing number of companies using sales staff to make the collection. This can be of value if the sales staff call frequently, such as the food industry, soft drink manufacturers or auto parts wholesalers. If commissioned salespeople are employed, it may be desirable to withhold commissions until the accounts are collected. This has an immediate effect on the collections. On the other hand, industry practice may not permit this.

When to start collection efforts

The collection effort starts when the account is opened. With large new accounts, a call should be made five to 10 days *before* the account is due to "welcome" the customer and ensure that the customer received the invoice, that the documentation is in order and that a cheque will be processed. This is not only excellent customer relations but trains the customer as well (aside from getting the cheque on time).

The normal collection process is part of the policy decisions that need to be made, for example, profit margins, industry practices, staffing needs, etc. Each of these areas will need to be analyzed. In some industries, a grace period of ten to fifteen days passes before a letter is sent, in others, a telephone call is made first, then letters.

Properly training the staff to make effective calls, and recognize danger signals, prepare rebuttals for excuses from customers, know the language of the courts (writ of execution, petition in bankruptcy, etc.) pays immense dividends. Most experienced collectors can sense when a customer is not going to pay. If the collection call has been done properly, whether this occurs when the account is one hour past due or 60 days, the collector knows that it is time for the next step in the process — a final letter, placing for collection or calling the company lawyer. All of this should be determined in advance.

Reminder

Notification of past due balances is the second step and can be referred to as the *reminder stage*. While the telephone is the most useful tool, most companies lack the staff to call all accounts which are one to ten days past due. For some reason, the staff is always available to call accounts that are 120 days past due but not the current ones. In any event, the reminder stage can be accomplished with stickers or requests printed on statements. Reminders shuld not offend, and encouragement should be gentle but at the same time professional. The main point is to convey the concern of the seller to the buyer. The next routine reminder, either by telephone or by written notification should be sent no later than five days after the preliminary reminder. However, because of the inconsistency of mail delivery, ten days may be a better choice.

The objective of reminder notices is not only to collect the money but also to test the customer's intentions. Creditors tend to be placed into three categories:

1. Those that demand and expect to get paid on time;
2. Those that will let us be a little slow from time to time; and
3. Those that don't seem to care.

Discussion

When reminders do not produce an appropriate response, that is, a cheque, it is time for discussion. This stage is a transition from the impersonal to a personal appeal for payment of the account. Collection letters have generally now been replaced by e-mail and phone calls. The use of "sales techniques" to collect produces the best results. A sales technique is the ability to come up with a reason why the customer, who is now a debtor, should pay today. This can be an appeal based on the credit rating (your credit rating is a valuable asset), or an appeal to reputation (you can still restore your credit reputation by paying your debt immediately) or a softer appeal to fair play (pointing out that the relationship has been like a partnership over many years).

Creating a script for a telephone call requires planning, an objective and prepared response for whatever the customer/debtor answers.

An example — "Mr. Smith, this is Janet Brown from Excelsior Plastics. I'm calling about the $4,414.67 that is now overdue. Mr. Smith, will you have a cheque ready for me to pick up this afternoon?"

Now, list all the common reasons why the bill hasn't been paid: no money, no cheques, can't collect own receivables, computer is broken, sales are down, and I'm expecting a big cheque next week. The list is endless, including the favourite — the cheque is in the mail.

The professional credit department will have researched all of the common excuses and have prepared rebuttals so that the collection call ends in a definite "yes" or a definite "no". It is necessary to test the intentions of the customer and be alert to danger signals. Suppose a customer says "I can't pay because I'm just changing banks", how does the collector respond? Should the account be sent to a lawyer or collection agency, even though it is not that old? The answer is that a professional collector will, at the end of the call, either have a promise of payment, a payment plan or the collector should proceed to the next step in the policy, whether it is collection or a lawsuit.

If letters are used, the letters should become forceful and give a date when further action will be taken. If the letter says ten days, then ten days is all that should pass, not 11 or 15. The customer/debtor has to understand that "we are a professional organization". Here are some examples:

Example 1

Unfortunately your account is at a point where it can no longer be tolerated. Therefore, should payment in full not be received in this office by November 20, your account will be assigned to our solicitors for collection. In so doing, your credit reputation will be irreparably harmed.

Example 2

We hereby issue a formal demand for payment of the following invoices:

Date	Invoice Number	Amount

Total amount outstanding: _____

If we do not receive payment in full or make acceptable arrangements with you by November 20, we will take whatever action we deem necessary to enforce collection.

This is our formal demand for payment, govern yourselves accordingly.

Example 3

Unfortunately you have left just one course open to us and that is, to take the necessary legal action to enforce payment. This is a great expense for both of us. Your cheque for $500 by November 20 will settle the matter.

If the effort exerted during the *discussion stage* fails to produce a satisfactory result, either a cheque or a payment plan, there is no choice left but to take drastic action. Restraint no longer needs to be practised, as the sole objective is to recover as much of the debt as possible. However, punitive action should only be taken if there is evidence that moneys or assets are available to satisfy the debt. A new credit investigation is often called for (but rarely done). It may be more desirable to write off the account than to pursue it if there is in fact no money available. Vengeance may be sweet but the potential expense is often not worth the effort.

Recovery

The discussion stage may end with arrangements for payment, post-dated cheques, promissory notes, securing the transaction, or even full payment.

If all efforts fail to successfully arrange for payment of the account, the last stage of the process occurs. The credit manager no longer has to practise good customer relations or restraint in his efforts, although as mentioned earlier, it may be more desirable to write off the account than proceed with punitive action. If, however, there is evidence that a portion or all of the account is recoverable, the following steps may be of help.

CANADIAN CASH MANAGEMENT

Collection Agencies

The use of collection agencies is common in Canada. Agencies range in size from small local firms dealing with companies whose accounts are confined to the local area to large national/international agencies who can collect accounts around the world. All agencies operate on the same basis, charging a fee on amounts collected. These fees vary according to the amount collected. The major agencies offer a free demand service of approximately ten days. A free demand service incorporates a final demand letter on the agency letterhead. If payment is made within the demand period, there is no fee. If payment is not received, further collection is commenced under normal fees.

Some agencies also offer demand letter services, utilizing word-processing to give every letter the "custom" look. These services may be purchased in a series of letters.

Some of the areas to be considered during the selection:

- Does the agency conform to the overall philosophy of the credit policies of your company? Agencies collect with different means. Some are softer in approach and are more capable of setting payment plans. Others are of the "knee-breaking" type, resorting to tactics such as feigning anger with the creditor and throwing the telephone into a nearby wastepaper basket for effect.
- Will the agency provide regular (at least once per month) reports on *all* accounts? This is very important. Some agencies are very neglectful in this area.
- How will collected funds be remitted? Once per month or less frequently?
- Does the agency provide Small Claims Court services?
- Can the agency collect in your entire trading area? Some smaller agencies forward accounts to other agencies or lawyers.

- How effective are they in collecting? Some are very proficient at selling their services, but collection skills are very weak.

Once again, overlapping your credit policies and philosophy can pay dividends when using a collection agency. In most cases, the cost of collection does not exceed the marginal revenue from the sale, and of course, the costs of bad debts greatly exceeds that of an agency.

When to use an agency or lawyer

Here are a few guidelines for placing with an agency or lawyer:

- When an NSF cheque is received and not made good within a few days.
- After three (or even two) broken promises for payment.
- When the customer/debtor appears to be avoiding any contact. Messages are not returned, decision maker is never in, etc.
- If time and effort being expended on collecting accounts could be put to better use, such as "training" every new customer.
- Finally, when your well-trained collector has resorted to all available in-house means.

Note that none of the above have anything to do with the age of the account. That is because an agency should be receiving accounts at any time that in-house means come to a standstill which could be at 31 days, or 180 days. The agency is another step in your process, not a dumping ground.

The final suggestion regarding collection agencies is to document your requirements and put them out to tender with a number of agencies. Rely on strategy rather than salesmanship.

Some creditors prefer to use the services of lawyers to effect their collection recovery. While many lawyers can be effective in sending letters on their letterhead, lawyers who are specialists in other means of collection are not found that frequently. Lawyers will usually charge a fee whether or not the account is collected.

Court Action

With the exception of Small Claims Court procedures, the issuance of a writ or statement of claim to effect payment will be carried out by a lawyer. It is important to realize that obtaining judgment does not automatically result in payment of the debt. If the company has little or no means to satisfy the obligation, it may be years before the claim can be settled. Bringing suit against a debtor produces adverse publicity for the defendant, which can also cause other creditors, particularly their banking sources, to review the existing lines of credit. The resulting reviews can cause an avalanche of other claims.

It is important, then, for the credit manager to do some homework before bringing suit. Does the debtor have assets or means to pay? Is the business a proprietorship or partnership, so that the personal assets can be attached? Are all proofs of delivery or documents proving the services were provided still available? Was a promissory note ever signed?

Small Claims Courts

Small Claims Courts are a useful avenue to collect smaller amounts. In most jurisdictions, the courts are "user friendly" and the use of lawyers is discouraged. The forms are easily filled out and for a nominal amount a Writ or Summons will be issued by the Court.

Maximum amounts collectable in small claims courts in canada

Alberta	$4,000
British Columbia	$10,000
Manitoba	$5,000
New Brunswick	$3,000
Newfoundland	$3,000
Northwest Territories	$5,000
Nova Scotia	$5,000
Ontario	$6,000
Prince Edward Island	$5,000
Quebec	$3,000
Saskatchewan	$5,000
Yukon	$5,000

There are differences in Small Claims Courts in each jurisdiction (as well as all other court procedures). In British Columbia, for example, it is possible to issue a Garnishing Order before judgment.

Some of the larger collection agencies dealing nationally have Small Claims Court Departments and the facilities to handle out-of-province claims.

Appendix 15A

Example application for credit

Legal name of company	Trade name (if any)	
Street address		Postal code
City and province		Telephone
Nature of business (please specify)		
Date business started	Monthly credit requirements $	
Building owned ( ) Rented ( )	Are you a subsidiary? If so name parent company	
Full names of directors or partners 1	Address	
2		
3		
4		
Full names of officers and shareholders if a corporation (attach details) President	Address	
Vice-president		
Secretary		
Treasurer	Branch and account number	
Name of bank		
Name of bank manager	Telephone	
Trade references and address 1		
2		
3		
Please attach set of financial statements		

TERMS OF CREDIT (30 days net)

All merchandise must be paid for in full within 30 days of date of each invoice, failing which an interest charge will be levied at the rate of 2% per month on all overdue accounts.

PURCHASER'S SIGNATURE
ACCEPTED BY_____

on_____

VENDOR'S SIGNATURE

Appendix 15B

Internal procedures checklist

Credit Approval	Yes	No	N/A	Comments
1. Is a written application required?				
2. Is there a standard form for credit applications?				
3. Are applicants checked out with a credit bureau?				
4. Does the evaluation consider bank credit history?				
5. Does the evaluation consider bank references?				

Invoices	Yes	No	N/A	Comments
1. Are invoices sent out promptly, not just at month-end?				
2. Is the invoice always accurate?				
3. Are payment terms clearly stated on the invoices?				
4. Are customers' special instructions followed carefully?				

Terms of Sale	Yes	No	N/A	Comments
1. Are the terms of payment clearly shown?				
2. Is the late payment penalty clearly shown?				

Statements	Yes	No	N/A	Comments
1. Are monthly statements submitted to all open accounts?				
2. Are statements prompt and accurate?				

Problem Identification	Yes	No	N/A	Comments
1. Is the average collection period calculated on a regular basis?				
2. Is the collection period compared with industry averages?				
3. Are changes to the collection period followed up?				
4. Is the collection period compared with payment terms?				
5. Is there a monthly aging of all outstanding accounts receivable?				
6. When a problem is identified, is corrective action prompt and firm?				

CREDIT AND COLLECTION

Follow-up	Yes	No	N/A	Comments
1. Is there a systematic procedure for follow-up on slow accounts?				
2. Is the telephone used to contact delinquent accounts?				
3. Is the telephone technique effective?				
4. Are there special procedures for collecting past-due accounts?				
5. Is there a late-payment penalty?				
6. Is an advance deposit required for seriously past due accounts?				

Cash Forecasting and Budgeting

Overview

Every company, no matter what size or industry, must carefully monitor its cash flow. Not paying attention to cash flow can result, at best, in lost opportunities for maximizing interest revenue or minimizing interest expense. At worst, it could result in illiquidity and, ultimately, insolvency.

Two basic tools for managing cash flow are cash forecasts and cash budgets, which are the subject of this chapter.

125

Cash Forecasts and Cash Budgets

A **cash forecast** is a schedule representing the most likely prediction of the sources and uses of cash for a particular period. It is usually prepared in blocks of time of one year initially, and then broken into shorter time periods. It shows details of the change in beginning to ending cash balance. Thus, it indicates reasons for expected fluctuations in the cash balance for the period under consideration. The net excess (deficiency) estimated after preparation of the forecast represents the increase (decrease) to the cash balance for the period.

A cash forecast plays an important role in carrying out the company's financial policy. For example, consideration must be given to dealing with excess cash. Should it be invested in short-term instruments such as treasury bills, used to reduce existing debt, or used for other purposes such as increased management bonuses? On the other hand, if the cash forecast indicates a deficit, then the deficit must be funded through, for example, increasing operational cash inflows, borrowing funds or issuing equity securities.

Because cash forecasts comprise a "best guess" as to cash flow activity and, in turn, affect investing and financing activity, they should not remain static. As information comes to light that renders the earlier cash flow assumptions incorrect, then the forecasts should be updated.

The purpose of a **cash budget** is to communicate the company's goals to employees and to motivate them to work towards meeting those goals. It does **not** represent what management believes is most likely to occur. The format and components of cash budgets will be the same as cash forecasts. However, the latter represents an ideal state of affairs, not necessarily the most likely scenario.

Both cash forecasts and budgets are often broken into daily, weekly, monthly, quarterly or semi-annual periods. More detailed forecasts and budgets for very short periods frequently are the most useful.

Importance of Forecasts and Budgets

Cash forecasts and budgets are important tools for financial managers in attaining the proper balance between safety (or liquidity) and profitability. They are necessitated by the objective of ensuring that adequate cash resources for day-to-day operations are maintained and excess resources are placed in adequately liquid investments earning some return. *The cash forecast and cash budget form part of the master budgeting and forecasting process that summarizes the company's plans and expectations for the upcoming period(s).*

Cash forecasts and cash budgets should play an integral role in helping to manage all of the company because:

- They ensure management, employees and the company are **focused**. It is an important step towards having all areas of the company (e.g., departments, divisions, etc.) work towards the same goals and to ensure management sets realistic goals.
- They help ensure business activities are **run effectively.** Cash forecasts predict whether cash will be required in various future periods to fund a shortfall in cash in advance of when those funds are needed. The treasurer can then negotiate to borrow funds or issue equity from a position of strength rather than under undue pressure. This, in turn, permits flexibility in searching for sources of funds and will lower the cost of financing operations. If the cash forecast indicates excess funds, you will have sufficient time to assess the most suitable sources in which to invest and,

therefore, earn a return. In addition, cash planning helps to coordinate the activities of the entire company.

- Cash budgets help **motivate employees** to meet established goals. If goals are realistic and employees are involved in the planning stage, they are more likely to work towards meeting goals.

- They provide a **measure of control** for performance evaluation purposes. Actual performance should be measured against cash budgets at selected intervals. The nature of discrepancies needs to be investigated and corrective action taken if thought necessary. This measure of control is necessary for all levels of the entity (e.g., divisions, projects, etc.).

- They often are **required by lenders before funds can be obtained.** For example, banks and other financial institutions will want to know how the company plans to repay a loan before funds are committed and advanced. Similarly, before issuing securities to the public, a prospectus, approved by the appropriate provincial securities commission(s), must be produced and distributed. Depending on the requirements of the relevant securities commission, this prospectus may have to include a multi-year projected income statement and balance sheet (for which the cash position must be forecast). In addition, supplemental schedules of forecast cash flow often are included.

Thus, one objective is to show potential creditors or investors that your company has a viable, well-thought out plan for putting funds requested to profitable use. Another objective is to indicate that orderly repayment (in case of debt) is feasible, or reasonable returns in the form of dividends or other items (in the case of other securities) is likely.

Because most companies use accrual-based accounting and reporting systems, it is important to ensure that goals, activities and evaluations relevant to the cash forecasts and budgets are consistent with those used in the accrual-based reporting system.

Preparing Cash Forecasts

In general, past results (actual or estimated actual, if actual is not yet available) are the starting point for preparing cash forecasts. However, you should recognize that past results are not necessarily and not usually indicative of what will happen in the future. Therefore, consideration must be given to existing and anticipated environmental factors (e.g., economy, industry, etc.).

Preparing forecasts and budgets for several years or periods can be extremely time-consuming. Either general spreadsheet programs or specialized software may be used. The latter can perform the forecast and budget calculations as well as scenario analysis once the assumptions and relationships among data are specified. Such programs may permit faster preparation of forecasts and budgets, more extensive scenario analysis and the ability to react quickly to unexpected situations as they develop.

It is important that various levels of knowledgeable personnel be involved in the cash forecasting and budgeting processes. Senior management, which often has a significant amount of experience in the industry and sees the "big picture", should have input into the preparation of the forecasts and budgets.

The steps required to prepare a cash forecast are set out below and illustrated in a comprehensive example that starts on page 143.

1. Forecast revenue schedule

The first step is to forecast revenue on an accrual basis and prepare the forecast revenue schedule. This is the most important step as other items affecting the cash forecast generally are derived based on revenue figures. For example, revenue estimates will have a significant effect on planned purchases, estimated cost of revenue budget, accounts receivable figures, etc.

Different approaches to preparing the revenue forecast include the following:

(a) An *internal approach* relies on the knowledge base within the company to forecast revenues. Sales/marketing personnel prepare forecasts based on their area of product specialization. The marketing/sales manager reviews these estimates. The general starting point for these employees is consideration of prior years' revenue.

(b) The *external approach* begins with a consideration of general economic conditions and the condition of the particular industry under consideration. Total industry revenue is first projected. Your company's market share then is estimated by considering such factors as historical market shares, new companies entering into the industry, planned competitive strategies, etc. Finally, the forecast is broken into product lines.

(c) The preferable approach is a combination of the internal and external approaches. A single approach should never be used since the business environment is too dynamic. Instead, revenue forecasts can be prepared under each approach and differences then reconciled.

In preparing revenue forecasts, factors such as the following should be considered:

- *General and industry economic conditions* — For example, in a recession, industries manufacturing and selling necessities such as food perform well. However, companies involved in producing and marketing luxury items such as cars, appliances and real estate-related products do not.
- The *amount and pattern of past revenue* (e.g., by product line, geographic area, salesperson).
- *Predictions of marketing personnel.*
- *Existing marketing campaign plans.*
- *Competitors* — What are the strengths and weaknesses of competitors compared to your company? What effect have they had on recent results of your company? What are their plans?
- *Expected price changes* — Anticipated price increases and decreases should be reflected in the forecast. The effect of unit price changes on unit sales needs to be assessed as well. For example, a 10 per cent increase in sales prices may result in a 20 per cent decline in unit sales. In this case, revenue would be lower than the prior year.
- *Product line plans for the company* — For example, are new products planned to come on-line during the forecast period? Is production of certain current products expected to be stopped?
- *Revenue budgets,* if already prepared.

It is important to ensure that all assumptions used to develop the revenue forecast are consistent with an accrual basis of accounting, not a cash basis. (Step 3 converts accrual-based figures to the cash basis.)

A revenue forecast should be prepared for both number of units and dollar volume of revenue. You should prepare the forecast under various "what if" scenarios since projections of any kind are purely judgemental and not all factors affecting revenue can be accurately predicted.

"What if" or scenario analysis is very useful in assessing the effect of changes in different variables affecting revenue (as well as other items). Preparing and analyzing the effect of various possible revenue figures helps ensure the corporation is equipped to react to actual results. Such analysis can indicate potential areas of concern as well as areas of opportunity.

Detailed month-by-month revenue forecasts, rather than summarized or annual forecasts, should be prepared. This will aid in preparing month-by-month detailed cash forecasts. This is particularly important for seasonal operations (e.g., the retail industry).

Information for forecasts of any kind should be prepared by, or with significant input from, the most knowledgeable individuals in the company. Therefore, in producing revenue forecasts, the marketing department should be involved in the departments. If an employee knowledgeable in economics exists in your company, he or she will be an invaluable reference point. If not, external sources should be consulted. For example, economic predictions such as interest rates and housing starts should be obtained. Such information is available from large financial institutions that have economic research departments as well as from investment dealers. Statistics Canada has a vast array of historical information available which may be useful in the process. Other sources of information include industry associations and the general media (e.g., newspapers and periodicals).

Once the revenue forecast is prepared, consideration must be given as to whether the figures are realistic. For example, if expected revenue looks too low, consideration should be given to various methods of increasing revenue as well as the likelihood of the company undertaking such plans. If such plans are likely, the revenue forecast should be revised.

2. Detailed cost schedules

The second step is to estimate various costs/expenses on an accrual basis and prepare detailed schedules for each category of items. Some cost-revenue relationships may be linear and therefore, easy to predict based on past experience. For example, if a company has no plans for expansion or cost-cutting measures, personnel costs may be calculated based on expected revenue levels (per Step 1 above). However, more often than not, relationships among revenue and cost items will not be that apparent. In addition, historical references should not be simply accepted before understanding why those relationships existed and whether they are still applicable. For example, the company's strategic plan, changing regulations, changing industry structure and competitiveness and economic conditions should be considered.

It is important to ensure that all assumptions used to develop the revenue forecast must be consistent with an accrual basis of accounting, not a cash basis. (Step 3 converts accrual-based figures to the cash basis.)

Regression analysis and other statistical tools may be useful in developing past relationships among financial statement items. However, the ultimate caveat regarding forecasts must be kept in mind: past relationships may not, and are not likely to, continue in the future.

Past relationships of cost of revenue to revenue often can be used to establish a reasonable estimate for forecasting purposes. However, many companies with complex cost structures will need to analyze in detail each component of the cost of revenue (e.g., direct labour, direct material, overhead items such as indirect labour, supplies, rent, depreciation). As well, cost of revenue in the case of companies that produce goods will have to be allocated between ending inventory and cost of revenue.

There may be a direct and well understood relationship between selling/marketing expense and revenue. However, the company's marketing thrust and the competitive environment must be considered to determine if this relationship is still applicable.

A company with fixed interest rates on its debt (e.g., bonds, certain bank financing) can easily forecast interest expense. However, due to recent experience with significantly fluctuating interest rates, many lenders will not, or generally do not, lend fixed rate funds. (There are, however, financial instruments such as interest rate swaps that permit fixing of interest rates on debt for a certain cost.) Therefore, it is important to research anticipated interest rates to project interest expense. Scenario analysis is especially useful because of the good possibility of changes (and possibly wide swings) in interest rates.

A company with foreign operations (e.g., subsidiaries, distribution centres, purchases) will have to consider expected exchange rates. Again, scenario analysis will be very useful. There are instruments that permit fixing exposure to foreign exchange fluctuations such as forward rate agreements and futures. If a company uses these, forecasting cash flows will be easier than otherwise.

Consideration of future tax rates (both federal and provincial), level of investment in fixed assets (which affects the amount of capital cost allowance permitted to reduce taxable income), anticipated revisions to tax legislation, and other factors needs to be made to estimate the amount of income taxes to be paid.

At the end of this step, various schedules will be prepared such as schedules of purchases, production, inventories, operating expenses, selling/marketing, and general and administrative. Again, it is important to recognize the significant increase in quality of forecast cost figures if knowledgeable individuals are involved in the forecasting process.

The starting point for both steps 1 and 2 is usually past operating results from a company's accrual-based reporting system. These results are then adjusted to reflect management's expectations for future operations.

3. Turning revenues and costs into cash flow equivalents

Revenue and expenses (as reflected on the income statement) rarely equal cash inflows and outflows. This is because customers often do not pay for goods and services immediately, and companies do not pay funds for goods and services used as the costs are recognized for accounting purposes. For example, employees earn their wages as the time clock ticks. However, they may only receive a paycheque biweekly. *Step 3 changes estimates of revenue and expenses on an accounting basis to the cash basis.* Modifying accrual-based estimates to the cash basis will likely require a reasonable amount of effort.

Completion of this step produces several schedules. Specifically, schedules of cash collections from customers, of cash disbursements for purchases, and of cash disbursements for operating expenses must be prepared.

The first stage in the process is to eliminate non-cash items that are shown as revenues, gains, expenses or losses on forecast schedules. Typical items include depreciation, amortization, gains and losses on the sale of capital assets and deferred income taxes.

Cash flow from operating activities should be calculated first. This will tell you how much cash is available for investing and financing purposes. If a shortage of cash from operations is indicated, available sources of cash (e.g., borrow from financial institutions, issue debt or equity securities, sell unnecessary capital assets, sell investment assets, sale/leaseback of capital assets, sell a division or subsidiary) must be considered.

The company's history of collections and payments should be assessed, as well as the likelihood of this experience continuing in the future. To begin, terms of credit should be reviewed and it should be determined through discussion with appropriate personnel whether changes are anticipated. For example, if credit terms are net 30, and customers typically pay their accounts within 35 days but a significant decline in economic conditions is expected, using a 35-day collection period for cash forecasts may not be reasonable. However, if collection efforts will likely increase (which would likely increase costs — this should be reflected on the cash forecast), the 35-day period may be appropriate.

If substantial revenue growth is expected, asset accounts are generally increased by a reasonable amount (e.g., inventory and accounts receivable). If real revenue growth is expected to continue, investment in capital assets (such as land, building, equipment) as well as employees will be necessary. Anticipated growth may be the result of increased physical volume revenues as well as inflationary price level increases. High inflation tends to force firms into the financial markets for funding; however, funding costs in a highly inflationary economy are expensive due to high interest rates.

The balance in various account categories such as accounts receivable and accounts payable must be estimated to support expected revenues. A linear or proportional relationship between revenues and accounts receivable likely will hold true if credit terms and economic conditions are expected to stay the same; however, past relationships must be reconsidered during each forecasting session.

4. Sources other than operating activities

Cash inflows and outflows related to sources other than operating activities must be estimated in this step. Cash flows can be affected significantly by activities other than the regular operations of the company. For example, cash inflows may arise during a particular year from the sale of subsidiaries, divisions or capital assets. Proceeds from insurance policies (cash inflows) may or may not adequately cover the expenditures necessitated by some disaster such as a fire or flood.

5. Investing cash flows (including capital expenditures)

The next step is to consider and analyze investing cash flow items. This step requires forecasting the extent of capital additions and disposals in the upcoming period(s). Forecasting of capital asset transactions is very important due to the high dollar value of cash receipts or payments that can result. In addition, capital asset transactions are often more discretionary than operations.

During this step, it must be considered whether or not certain investments must or should be made even if cash is not available. For example, certain equipment may need to be replaced to continue operating your business effectively no matter what the source of the funds is. If so, a decision about the likely mode of financing these investments is required in step 6.

Special consideration will have to be paid to expenditures which will be capitalized (i.e., recorded as an asset rather than as an expense). If, for example, interest and wage payments will be capitalized during the construction of a building, these cash outflows should be included in the cash forecast.

An estimate of dividends to be paid is required. The best starting point is past dividend payment policies. Then, expected cash flow from operations should be examined. If cash flow is estimated to be "tight", the desirability of paying dividends should be reconsidered and senior management consulted as to its views.

6. Excess or deficiency of cash before financings

The next step is to calculate the excess or deficiency of cash before financing activities. This calculation estimates what your company's financing needs are. If a deficiency is identified, consideration must be given to the most appropriate action (e.g., increase revenues, decrease payments). For example, management may decide that while expenditures are in line, there is room to increase revenue through enhancing marketing strategies.

If excess cash is anticipated, any revenues from investment of those funds will have to be calculated and included on the cash forecast.

7. Planned financing activities

The next step is to adjust the results to reflect planned financing activities. Possibilities include:

- *Borrowing funds* from a bank or other financial institution, or from the investing public (through an issue of debentures or bonds, for example). Important factors to include in the evaluation are the cost of borrowing, whether or not there are sources willing to lend money to the company, and the extent of current borrowings. If current borrowings are too high, increasing existing debt levels may put the successful future of your company in jeopardy.
- *Postponing payments* to creditors (e.g., trade accounts payable, bank loan). A key consideration here is the likelihood of upsetting important creditors and damaging future relationships.
- *Reducing discretionary expenses* such as advertising and management bonuses, and reducing staffing levels.
- *Reducing customers' credit terms or otherwise accelerating customer payments* to reduce accounts receivable collection time. This may not increase the turnover of accounts in recessionary times if customers are in tight cash positions themselves.
- *Postponing or accelerating planned capital expenditures.*
- *Postponing or increasing dividend payments.*
- Entering into *sale/leaseback transactions* to increase cash inflows.

Another item of consideration is whether a minimum cash balance is required as a measure of security. If so, this amount should be included when calculating the level of financing required (i.e., reduce forecast cash surplus or increase cash deficit).

Cash outflows in the cash forecast will have to be adjusted for estimated interest costs, principal repayments and dividend payments based on the selected financing method(s).

Steps 1 through 7 should be repeated for different key assumptions until the desired plan is obtained. Performing adequate scenario analysis is very important since it is impossible to predict the future exactly or even fairly closely for most companies. (**Scenario analysis** is applying different "what if" possibilities to different key variables/assumptions affecting the cash forecast.) Therefore, you need to think through various alternatives that may transpire.

8. Compile the cash forecast

This step is simply a summary of steps 1 through 7. The objective is to summarize the information prepared in the previous seven steps for distribution to interested parties in your company.

9. Revise the cash forecast for new information

The process of forecasting cash flow is iterative and requires much thought and effort. Because no one can predict the exact combination of events that will occur in the future, forecasts will not be met. Therefore, they should be modified as new information becomes available; cash forecasting and budgeting should be considered a continuous process. To illustrate, if revenue for a given month was below expectations, management should reconsider whether the forecast for remaining months is appropriate or should be adjusted. Of course, there is a tradeoff between the benefits from more accurate forecasts, and the costs involved.

Preparing Cash Budgets

Once the cash forecast has been prepared, it should be modified as necessary to prepare the cash budget. During this process, the effect of various budget figures on the company must be considered. For example, budgets that obviously are not attainable may have a negative impact on employees instead of encouraging them to work harder to achieve the high standards. On the other hand, an easily attainable budget may result in employees not reaching their full potential, only that envisaged in the budget. Therefore, care must be taken to select the highest motivating budget.

The budget may be equal to the forecast at the start of the year. The budget would be fixed, whereas the forecast will be adjusted to reflect estimated actual figures.

After the budget has been prepared and communicated to various levels of the company, the next phase is to assess performance, analyze discrepancies and take any necessary corrective action. This phase involves comparing actual results to the cash budget. It serves as the control mechanism. Unless discrepancies are analyzed and corrective action implemented, a significant benefit of the cash budgeting process is lost.

You must assess the degree to which employees' compensation should be based on achieving budgeted results. In general, the more directly their remuneration is based on meeting budgets, the harder they will work towards meeting them. However, the extent to which employees are remunerated based on meeting their budgets should be determined by considering the achievability of the budgets.

Improving the Accuracy of Cash Forecasts and Budgets

The following suggestions will help to enhance the cash forecast and budget process:

- An *adequate amount of time* should be dedicated to the process. Also, the process should be started sufficiently early to permit appropriate consideration of all key variables.
- The forecast and budget should be *prepared by knowledgeable, experienced personnel.* Sound judgment plays an important role in the process. Input from those directly involved in line activities should be obtained.
- The forecast should be *broken down into very detailed components.* Analysis of assumptions at this level is necessary. For a cash forecast to be relatively accurate, the assumptions used to prepare the forecast must be of high quality.
- *Various scenarios should be applied.* The more scenarios used, the more likely the forecast and budget will be well-thought out plans that are useful to your company. Preparing cash forecasts and budgets is an iterative process. The results of one scenario often raises questions which need to be answered to fine-tune the forecast or budget.
- *Use spreadsheets or specialized software.* They permit quicker preparation of cash forecasts and budgets, and make additional scenario analysis more feasible. Software packages are available which permit the integration of an accrual-based reporting system with a cash forecasting and budgeting system.
- *Regression analysis* may be useful for developing relationships among variables and key accounts. Regression analysis is a statistical model that measures the average amount of change in a dependent variable that is associated with a unit change in the amount of one or more cost drivers.

CASH FORECASTING AND BUDGETING

There are various off-the-shelf software programs available to assist in performing regression analysis.

Summary

Preparing cash forecasts and budgets are a necessary and integral part of managing a company. The more time spent on developing forecasts and budgets, the more prepared a company will be for dealing with its dynamic environment.

Example

The following example illustrates the steps involved in preparing a cash budget as discussed above. It sets out a monthly forecast for a six-month period.

Step 1. Forecast revenue schedule

A company may forecast its revenue using the following format:

	Jan.	Feb.	March	April	May	June	Total
(in $000s)							
Cash revenue	$100	$150	$200	$100	$300	$250	$1,100
Credit revenue[1]	400	450	600	300	300	700	2,750
Total	$500	$600	$800	$400	$600	$950	$3,850

Major assumptions:
[1] On average, customers pay 50 per cent of the amount due within 30 days and the remainder within 60 days. Insignificant bad debts are expected. Credit revenue in December was $800.

Step 2. Forecast cost schedules

Once forecast revenue schedules are prepared, schedules detailing purchases and operating expenses can be prepared.

Purchases and Cost of Revenue:

(in $000s)	Jan.	Feb.	March	April	May	June	Total
Cost of revenue[1]	$300	$360	$480	$240	$360	$570	$2,310
Add: Desired ending inventory[2]	180	240	120	180	285	450	450
Less: Beginning inventory[3]	(200)	(180)	(240)	(120)	(180)	(285)	(200)
Purchases	280	420	360	300	465	735	2,560
GST	20	29	25	21	33	51	179
	$300	$449	$385	$321	$498	$786	$2,739

Major assumptions:

[1] Cost of revenue is 60 per cent of revenue. Excludes GST.
[2] Desired ending inventory is 50 per cent of cost of revenue for the next month. Cost of sales for July is expected to be $900.
[3] Beginning inventory for January is $200.

Operating Expenses:

(in $000s)	Jan.	Feb.	March	April	May	June	Total
Salaries, wages and benefits	$30	$30	$30	$30	$30	$30	$180
Commissions[1]	50	60	80	40	60	95	385
Personnel costs	80	90	110	70	90	125	565
Rent[2]	80	80	80	80	80	80	480
Depreciation	40	40	40	40	40	40	240
Insurance[3]	10	10	10	10	10	10	60
Miscellaneous	10	10	20	10	10	20	80
Total	$220	$230	$260	$210	$230	$275	$1,425

Major assumptions:

[1] Commissions paid to salespersons are 10 per cent of sales.

[2] Rent is paid in the month following its incurrence. December rent expense was $50.

[3] Insurance is paid in January for the entire year — $120.

Step 3. Turning forecasts into cash flow equivalents

A number of adjustments must be made to turn accounting-basis revenue and cost amounts to their cash flow equivalents.

Cash Collections from Customers:

	Jan.	Feb.	March	April	May	June	Total
(in $000s)							
Cash revenue[1]	$100	$150	$200	$100	$300	$250	$1,100
50% of current month's credit revenue[1]	200	225	300	150	150	350	1,375
50% of prior month's credit revenue[1]	400	200	225	300	150	150	1,425
	700	575	725	550	600	750	3,900
GST and provincial sales tax collected	75	105	85	105	80	90	540
Total	$775	$680	$810	$655	$680	$840	$4,440

Notes:

[1]   From Step 1.

Operating Expenditures:

(in $000s)	Jan.	Feb.	March	April	May	June	Total
Expenses[3]	$220	$230	$260	$210	$230	$275	$1,425
Adjustments							
Depreciation[3]	(40)	(40)	(40)	(40)	(40)	(40)	(240)
Rent[1]	(30)						(30)
Insurance[2]	110	(10)	(10)	(10)	(10)	(10)	60
Income tax instalments	50	50	50	50	50	50	300
	310	230	260	210	230	275	1,515
GST paid to suppliers	30	25	25	30	30	50	190
Total	$340	$255	$285	$240	$260	$325	$1,705

Major assumptions:

[1]   Rent is paid in the month following. December rent expense was $50.

[2]   Insurance is paid in January for the entire year — $120.

Notes:

[3]   From Step 2.

Steps 4 – 6. Estimate cash gains and losses; analyze investing cash flow items; calculate excess/deficiency of cash before financing

Before considering financing activities, the information from steps 1, 2 and 3 must be compiled, and other items affecting cash considered.

(in $000s)

	Jan.	Feb.	March	April	May	June
Beginning cash balance[1]	$50	$100	$99	$102	$100	$97
Cash receipts:						
Customers[3]	775	680	810	655	680	840
Sale of land[3]					950	
Cash available **A**	825	780	909	757	1,730	937
Cash payments						
Purchases[2]	500	280	420	360	300	465
Operating costs before GST[3]	310	230	260	210	230	275
GST and provincial sales tax paid to suppliers[4]	50	54	50	51	63	101
GST remitted or refunded[5]	40	25	51	35	54	17
Dividends	50					
Capital acquisitions					100	
Total **B**	950	589	781	656	747	858
Minimum cash balance desired	100	100	100	100	100	100
Total cash needs	1,050	689	881	756	847	958
Net cash excess (deficiency) before financing	$(225)	$91	$28	$1	$883	$(21)

Major assumptions:

1. January 1 cash balance was $50.
2. Credit terms from suppliers are n/30. The company does not pay suppliers before the due date. December purchases were $500.

Notes:

3. From Step 3. Includes GST.
4. From Steps 2 and 3.
5. Difference between GST and PST collected from customers and GST paid to suppliers (per Steps 2 and 3 schedules). Net GST and PST owed to (from) the government is remitted (received) one month following the month of collection. At the beginning of January, $40 was owed for these taxes.

Step 7. Reflect planned financing

A company may have decided it requires financing prior to the cash forecasting exercise. However, through forecasting its cash flows, a company may find it needs financing to achieve its future goals.

(in $000s)	Jan.	Feb.	March	April	May	June
Financing[1]						
Borrowings[2]	$225	$0	$0	$0	$0	$0
Principal payments[3]	0	(90)	(25)	0	(110)	0
Interest payments[2]	0	(2)	(1)	(1)	(1)	0
Net financing effect	$225	$(92)	$(26)	$(1)	$(111)	$0
Investing[4]						
Deposit excess cash	$0	$0	$0	$0	$(775)	$0
Interest earned	0	0	0	0	0	6
Liquidate investments	0	0	0	0	0	15
Net investing effect	$0	$0	$0	$0	$(775)	$21
Net cash excess (deficiency) before financing **A–B**	$(125)	$191	$128	$101	$983	$79
Net financing effect	$225	(92)	(26)	(1)	(111)	0
Net investing effect	0	0	0	0	(775)	21
Cash balance, end of month	$100	$99	$102	$100	$97	$100

Major assumptions:

[1] The company does not need to borrow until month-end.

[2] The company has arranged a $250,000 line of credit at 12 per cent before or during January that requires only interest payments to be made during the first year. Borrowings must be in $5,000 blocks. Interest is rounded to the nearest $1,000.

[3] Repayments to be made at month-end, and must be in $5,000 blocks.

[4] An interest rate of 9 per cent could be earned in short-term investments that are cashable every 30 day period. Deposits are made at month-end, interest is receivable monthly at the end of the following month and investments can only be made in $5,000 blocks.

Step 8. Compilation of the cash flow forecast

Following is the result of the previous steps in a presentable format:

(in $000s)	Jan.	Feb.	March	April	May	June
Cash receipts:						
Customers[1]	$700	$575	$725	$550	$600	$750
GST and PST collected[1]	75	105	85	105	80	90
Sale of land[2]					950	
Borrowings[3]	225	0	0	0	0	0
Interest on short-term investments[3]	0	0	0	0	0	6
Liquidate investments[3]	0	0	0	0	0	15
Total cash receipts	1,000	680	810	655	1,630	861
Cash payments:						
Purchases[2]	500	280	420	360	300	465
Personnel costs[5]	80	90	110	70	90	125
Rent[5]	50	80	80	80	80	80
Insurance[5]	120					
Miscellaneous[5]	10	10	20	10	10	20
Income tax instalments[1]	50	50	50	50	50	50
GST paid to suppliers[5]	50	54	50	51	63	101
GST and PST remitted to the government[2]	40	25	51	35	54	17
Dividends[2]	50					
Principal repayments[3]		90	25		110	
Interest payments[3]		2	1	1	1	
Acquire investments[3]					775	
Capital aquisitions[3]	0	0	0	0	100	0
Total cash payments	950	681	807	657	1,633	858
Net cash inflow (outflow)	50	(1)	3	(2)	(3)	3
Beginning cash balance	50	100	99	102	100	97
Ending cash balance	$100	$99	$102	$100	$97	$100

Notes:

[1]   From Step 3.
[2]   From Steps 4 – 6.
[3]   From Step 7.
[4]   From Step 2.
[5]   From Steps 2 and 3.

Index

The following references appear with their corresponding page numbers in Canadian Cash Management: A Guide to Financial Strategies.

Debit cards, 70

E-commerce
accounts payable, 66
accounts receivables, 67
Automated Clearance Settlement System, 59
Automated teller machine (ATM), 52
Canadian Payments Association (CPA), 58
debit card, 70
defined, 54
electronic data interchange, 56
Electronic Funds Transfer (EFT), 51
electronic money, 73
emerging technology, 69
extending credit, 95
internet, 72
large value transaction system (LVTS), 62
mondex, 69
origins, 52
outside Canada, 80
p.c. banking, 72
payments, 57, 77
processes for business, 53
procurement cards, 78
proxy-based services, 74
reporting, 79
smart cards, 69
standards, 75
telephone banking, 71
Electronic data interchange. *See* **E-commerce and payments**
Emerging technology, 69

Financial strategy, 1
corporate mission, 1